StarGuard

Best Practices for Lifeguards

THIRD EDITION

Jill E. White

Starfish Aquatics Institute

HUMAN
KINETICS

Library of Congress Cataloging-in-Publication Data

White, Jill E., 1955-
    Starguard : best practices for lifeguards / Jill E. White.-- 3rd ed.
        p. cm.
        Includes bibliographical references.
    ISBN 0-7360-6075-8 (soft cover)
    1. Lifeguards--Training of--Handbooks, manuals, etc. I. Title.
    GV838.74.W45 2006
    797.2'1'0289--dc22

                                                    2005022896

ISBN-10: 0-7360-6075-8 (print)   ISBN-10: 0-7360-8587-4 (Adobe PDF)
ISBN-13: 978-0-7360-6075-2 (print)   ISBN-13: 978-0-7360-8587-8 (Adobe PDF)

The Web addresses cited in this text were current as of November 2005, unless otherwise noted.

Acquisitions Editor: Patricia Sammann; **Developmental Editor:** Anne Cole; **Assistant Editor:** Bethany J. Bentley; **Copyeditor:** Annette Pierce; **Proofreader:** Jim Burns; **Permission Manager:** Carly Breeding; **Graphic Designer:** Nancy Rasmus; **Graphic Artist:** Sandra Meier; **Photo Manager:** Dan Wendt; **Cover Designer:** Keith Blomberg; **Photographer (cover):** Dan Wendt; **Photographer (interior):** Dan Wendt, except where otherwise noted. Photos on pages 5, 6 (top), 7, 28 (bottom), 110, 120, 135, 136 (top), 140, 143, and 148 © i Stock International Inc. Photo on page 6 (bottom) courtesy of Timber Ridge Lodge at Grand Geneva Resort. Photos on pages 14 (bottom), 31, 41, 47, 60, 76, 78 (bottom), 86, 88, 89, 90, 91, 118, 120, 129, 130, 131, 133, 144, 151, 153, 154, and 155 © Jill E. White. Photo on page 52 courtesy of Swimguard USA. Photos on pages 136 (bottom), 149, and 150 © Justin S. Padgett; **Art Manager:** Kareema McLendon; **Illustrator:** Argosy; Image on page 53 courtesy of Swimguard USA; **Printer:** Versa Press

Published by Human Kinetics, Inc., in cooperation with Starfish Aquatics Institute.

Printed in the United States of America   10   9   8   7   6

Human Kinetics
Web site: www.HumanKinetics.com

United States: Human Kinetics
P.O. Box 5076
Champaign, IL 61825-5076
800-747-4457
e-mail: humank@hkusa.com

Canada: Human Kinetics
475 Devonshire Road Unit 100
Windsor, ON N8Y 2L5
800-465-7301 (in Canada only)
e-mail: orders@hkcanada.com

Europe: Human Kinetics
107 Bradford Road
Stanningley
Leeds LS28 6AT, United Kingdom
+44 (0) 113 255 5665
e-mail: hk@hkeurope.com

Australia: Human Kinetics
57A Price Avenue
Lower Mitcham, South Australia 5062
08 8372 0999
e-mail: info@hkaustralia.com

New Zealand: Human Kinetics
P.O. Box 80
Torrens Park, South Australia 5062
0800 222 062
e-mail: info@hknewzealand.com

E3557

Contents

PART IV Aquatic Rescue

PART V Professionalism and Personal Safety

PART VI Site-Specific Considerations

Preface

Being a lifeguard is one of the most important jobs you'll ever have. Because you are responsible for helping aquatic facility patrons stay safe and healthy and for rescuing and helping them when accidents or disasters strike, you must be alert at all times. Because you may be called upon to save lives, you must keep your skills at rescue-ready levels at all times.

This doesn't mean that every moment on the job will be action packed. You will spend a lot of your lifeguarding time continuously concentrating on your assigned part of the pool, and that can get boring. But keeping alert and watching closely means that you can intervene by enforcing rules that help prevent drownings, injuries, and illnesses before they occur. Constantly watching the water also allows you to see an emergency early so that you can respond quickly and provide care.

The StarGuard program will develop your confidence and competence as a lifeguard. The information is concise and clear. Together, the text and the course teach you the essentials of lifeguarding by focusing on what is important.

StarGuard training also will develop the physical skills you need to perform swimming and rescue techniques. Although you will read about these skills in the text, you must actually practice them in training sessions taught by StarGuard instructors through a network of authorized training centers. Emergency care skills using the American Safety and Health Institute's curricula for CPR for the professional rescuer, first aid, bloodborne pathogens, emergency oxygen, and automated external defibrillation are integrated into the StarGuard training program. When you complete both the knowledge and skills components of the training, your professional skills will reach far above common standards.

This StarGuard text is divided into six parts:

- Part I   Prevention
- Part II   Surveillance
- Part III   Emergency Care
- Part IV   Aquatic Rescue
- Part V   Professionalism and Personal Safety
- Part VI   Site-Specific Considerations

Parts I through V are based on the Starfish Risk Management Model and explain the fundamentals of lifeguarding. Part VI provides supplemental information for lifeguards working at waterparks, on waterfronts, or in a wilderness setting.

In part I we talk about your role as a lifeguard in helping to prevent aquatic accidents. This includes understanding why it is important to know the objectives and best practices for lifeguarding, understanding aquatic risk management, knowing how to prevent transmission of bloodborne and waterborne illnesses, and applying common strategies for injury prevention.

In part II, we turn to specific and proven strategies you can use when scanning for potential problems. This is known as *surveillance* and is one of the most crucial lifeguarding skills. We start by describing distressed and drowning swimmers and the drowning process, then explain the best practices for how to scan zones, how to scan effectively, and how to stay alert.

Part III is a supplement to the text you will be provided for your American Safety and Health Institute emergency care training. Here we explain how to contact emergency medical systems, and we look at the specifics of first aid in and around an aquatic environment, including managing spinal injuries on land.

It is in part IV that we focus on the objectives and best practices for aquatic rescue. This includes assists and rescues for persons that are conscious, management of spinal injuries in the water, and rescue of unconscious drowning victims.

In part V we talk about best practices for personal health and safety as well as professionalism. In part VI we provide information about the unique lifeguarding challenges of waterparks and waterfront and wilderness environments. Several appendixes offer sample forms and reports.

To be a competent lifeguard, you must know more than just what you should do and how to perform isolated rescue skills. To be competent, you must be able to execute—to put all the pieces together and perform when you are on duty. The StarGuard program, which integrates information on how to lifeguard with the actions you will actually perform when you are lifeguarding, teaches the best practices that translate into saving lives. The course uses a hands-on teaching method called experiential learning. When learning through this method, you will have the opportunity to participate in scenarios that simulate situations similar to what you will experience on the job. You will be expected to know the objective for what you need to accomplish and integrate your skills and knowledge into solving the problem. Experiential learning is one of the most effective ways to develop confidence that carries over into real-life situations.

For StarGuard or StarReview information, contact:

Starfish Aquatics Institute
National Office and Aquatic Center
7240 Sallie Mood Drive
Savannah, GA 31406
912-692-1173
www.starfishaquatics.org

The terms used in this text for *drowning, drowning victim, drowning survivor,* and *drowning fatality* are based on definition guidelines developed at the World Congress on Drowning (WCOD) and approved in October, 2002, at a meeting of the International Liaison Committee on Resuscitation (ILCOR). (See definitions on pages 38 and 39.)

The term *lifeguard* generally refers to a person primarily responsible for monitoring patron behavior in an aquatic environment by providing constant, dedicated surveillance and enforcing the facility's preventive strategies.

The terms *rescuer* and *responder* generally refer to a person providing emergency care either in or out of the water. The terms may apply to a lifeguard who is responding to an emergency as well as to other aquatic personnel and bystanders who are assisting.

The terms *swimmer* and *patron* refer to people who are in or near the water at an aquatic facility.

The protocols presented in the StarGuard course for caring for unconscious persons or drowning victims are based on the guidelines from the 2005 International Consensus on Cardiopulmonary Resuscitation (CPR) and Emergency Cardiovascular Care (ECC) Science and Treatment Recommendations (CoSTR).

Operational recommendations in this text do not replace those of local or state regulatory agencies, such as state health departments. Always consult your local regulatory agency's guidelines, which should be considered to be primary.

The information in the StarGuard text and course is consistent with current and accepted guidelines and best practices, and provides suggestions for procedures and protocols. The circumstances of each incident will vary, and guidelines for aquatic safety and emergency care that will apply exactly in all cases do not exist. The publisher and authors make no representations or warranties with respect to any implied future performance by persons completing StarGuard training.

Lifeguard training and certification is simply the first step in becoming a competent lifeguard. The documentation you receive upon successfully completing the course verifies that you had certain skills and understanding at that time. The responsibility for future performance lies with you, your supervisor, manager, and employer.

The Starfish Aquatics Institute is committed to helping aquatic managers and employers of lifeguards maintain high standards. We offer a comprehensive aquatic risk management service plan that can provide lifeguard performance audits (StarReview) and operational support. The facility where you work may have this plan in place, in which case you can be assured that your employer is committed to the highest level of aquatic safety.

Acknowledgments

The Starfish Aquatics Institute would like to acknowledge the contributions of the following people to this book.

The first and second editions of this text were developed through a joint effort of the Starfish Aquatics Institute and the American Safety & Health Institute. Members of the Program Advisory Committee (PAC) and those that provided external review included: Lynn Alexander—Leeds Consulting; David Barney, Bryan Munsey, Melissa Reider, Lake White, Jennifer White, and Robbin White—The Champion Corporation; Natalie Bolten and Ellen Etling—Midwest Pool Management; Robert Clayton, EdD; Richard Clinchy III, PhD—Strategic Resources Alliance, Inc.; Heather Cummings, Janis Keim, and MaryBeth Pavoggi—City of Cape Coral Yacht Club; Janis K. Doleschal—Milwaukee Public Schools; Gerald Dworkin—Lifesaving Resources, Inc.; Ari Eisenberg, NREMT-P; Will Evans—Markel Insurance Company; Carol Lee Fick, RN—Jeff Ellis & Associates, Inc (retired); Mike Fischer and Tony Marzullo—City of Cape Coral Sunsplash Family Waterpark; Jeff Fryer—River Road Park & Recreation District; Ann Gisriel and Helen Whelan—Maryland Athletic Club; Barbara Law-Heitzman; Rob Jacobsen—Aquatics Galore; Jeffrey L. King—Aqua-Rec Management; Rea Kulick—TCA Clubs Forest Grove; Jed Livingstone—Professional Association of Diving Instructors (PADI); Steve Locke—USA Triathlon; John M. Malatak—United States Coast Guard; Ryan McAlister—Lake Shore Country Club; Wayne Mitchell—Walt Disney World; Chris Moler—Oklahoma City Community College; Lisbeth Moore—Boys & Girls Clubs of America; Noelle Navarro and Josh Ploch—DRD Pool Management; Earl Ostrander—SafetyWatch; Mark Ostrander—Public Safety Solutions; Jose V. Salazar, MPH, NREMT-P—Jose Salazar & Associates; Jane Storm, MS, RN—Pocono Medical Center; Chris Stephenson—Sunshine Aquatics; Tammy Tatum—Central Virginia Safety Concepts; Anne M. Wall—Marketing Navigators; Tom Werts—Aquatic Safety Consulting, Inc.; Ed Wilcox—Boy Scouts of America; Carol Fosdick Wright—Harvard Ridge; and Joseph P. Ziegler—NY State Office of Children and Family Services.

The Wilderness Program Advisory Committee (PAC) was led by Chair Justin S. Padgett, MS, NREMT-P, Landmark Learning, LLC. Members and external reviewers included: John David Early—Eastern Washington University; Mike Fischesser—The American Adventure Service Corps; Dave Hus—North Carolina Outward Bound School; Will Leverette—Affiliation of Risk Managers for Recreation; Dave Mason—American Canoe Association Dixie Division; Maurice Phipps PhD—Wilderness Education Association; Slim Ray—Rescue 3 International; and Steve Teixiera—Camp Woodson.

We are grateful to the individuals and agencies that have provided input toward meeting regulatory requirements: Steven Binns—Ohio Department of Health; Brett Davis and Kevin Hoffman—Park District Risk Management Association; Cathy Durance—USA Swimming; USA Swimming Safety Education Committee; Kendall Dunham and Douglas Sackett—State of New York Department of Health; Steve Elmer and David St. Jules—State of Wisconsin Department of Health and Family Services; Gary Fraser—State of Washington Department of Health; James Hayes—North Carolina Department of Environment and Natural Resources; Pat Hammond—American Camping Association; Stephen B. Keifer—Oregon Department of Human Services; Paul Klouse and Edmund Wojcik—Clark County Health District; Pat Metz—Illinois Department of Public Health; Robert Pryor—Florida Department of Health; the Lifeguard Advisory Committee; L. James Ridge—South Carolina Department of Health and Environmental Control; David T. Roberts—Maryland Department of Health and Mental Hygiene; Melinda Scarborough—Georgia Department of Human Resources/Environmental Health; Howard Wensley—The Commonwealth of Massachusetts Department of Public Health; and Dennis C. Wilson—Pennsylvania Department of Health; Drew Leemon and John Gookin—National Outdoor Leadership School.

We would like to acknowledge the professional contributions of Tom Griffiths, EdD; John McGovern, JD; Robert E. Ogoreuc, MEd; Peter J. Safar, MD; and Kim Tyson, MS.

We extend special appreciation to the management and staff of the Chatham County Aquatic Center, Savannah Yacht Club, Sunsplash Family Waterpark, Town of Ft. Myers Beach Pool, and Glenview Park District. We thank Steve Cable—Willamalane Parks & Recreation District; Mairi S. Padgett and Nathan Nahikian—Landmark Learning, LLC; Christopher Stec—Falling Creek Camp; and Marie Sheba, for assistance or contributions to this project.

Special thanks to Gregg Rich, Tim Eiman, Ralph Schenefelt, and Frank Swiger of the American Safety & Health Institute for an excellent working relationship. We are extremely grateful for the exceptional strategic guidance and wisdom that has been provided to Starfish Aquatics by the executive advisory board including Rob Bowden, Robert Clayton, Leslie Donavan, Carol L. Fick, Bert Forde, Adolph Kiefer, Rainer Martens, and Anne M. Wall, and excellent staff support provided by Lili McGovern, Brian White, Lake White, and Robbin White.

Prevention

Objectives

Knowledge	Skills	Execution
After reading part I, you should understand the following:	After hands-on or in-water practice, you should be able to demonstrate the following:	After scenario and site-specific training, you should be able to do the following:
The importance of early intervention Events or actions that can lead to drowning The Starfish risk management model Risk factors in an aquatic environment The Starfish layers-of-protection model The important role of the lifeguard The RID factor The diverse working environments for lifeguards The need for site-specific training The need for mutual responsibility in preventing injury or drowning How to reduce risk while testing swimming skills The importance of scene safety and isolating bodily substances The concept of universal precautions and use of personal protective equipment (PPE) Techniques for controlling exposure to and cleaning up bodily fluids The importance of patron education in preventing recreational water illnesses Guidelines for electrical safety How to monitor severe weather conditions The need for and techniques to enforce rules and policies The importance of identifying hazards The components of an emergency action plan How to provide directions to a crowd	Use of personal protective equipment Putting latex or vinyl gloves onto wet hands Removal of latex or vinyl gloves Cleanup of vomit, blood, and fecal matter	Isolate and clean up bodily substances as regulated by your state health department or following Center for Disease Control (CDC) guidelines Enforce rules and policies in a positive manner Identify hazards

Lifeguard Best Practices

Water hides and water suffocates. These two indisputable facts should never be far from your mind as you lifeguard. The potential for serious brain damage or death by drowning is never more than a few minutes away for anyone who is in the water. Swimming is a high-risk activity, and once a person slips beneath the water's surface no one may be aware that a drowning is taking place.

Swimming and water play are popular recreational activities, but, because they are fun, people tend to overlook the risk. Parents and caregivers often take the view that a visit to the pool or waterpark is their relaxation too, and become distracted. This complacency may also be accompanied by a misdirected attitude that the lifeguards are solely responsible for their children. Consider this "what if" example: What if you put an alligator in your pool? You keep it well fed, and it sleeps in a cage at the bottom of the pool. The chances of the alligator escaping are very low. How many parents would send their children to your pool? Probably none! Those same parents, however, don't realize that the water's ability to hide and suffocate a child is just as dangerous as keeping a live alligator on the bottom of the pool. If a child gets in water that is just a little too deep, or swallows a mouthful of water and is unable to cry out for help, the child can slip silently beneath the surface, unable to breathe. He or she may possibly be hidden from view by the glare of the sun or by other patrons, and no one notices the child is missing until it is too late.

The Best Practice Approach to Lifeguarding

A best practice is a method of performing that has been proven to be successful. A best practice approach to lifeguarding will help you focus on what is universally important. These proven best practices will be presented throughout this book and summarized at the end of each chapter. It is also important for you to understand the overall objective and goal of what you are trying to achieve by using the best practices. These, too, are summarized at the end of each chapter.

The role of a lifeguard has changed dramatically in the past decade. New technology such as automated external defibrillators (AED) and underwater surveillance systems and improved training opportunities have greatly expanded your ability as a lifeguard to provide care during an emergency. However, this expanded capability makes it tempting to lose sight of the vital element of lifeguarding that saves lives: A patron must be able to breathe to remain alive in the water. Despite the technology and new information, your focus is simple: Watch to see that patrons can breathe by making sure they remain on the surface of the water or are able to return to the surface after submerging.

We begin our discussion of best practices in lifeguarding by taking a quick look at the events that can lead to drowning, then look at the factors that could keep you from performing at your best. Finally, we consider the types of aquatic environments you might guard and their specific training requirements.

Events That Cause Drowning

For a drowning to occur, a person's face and airway must be covered with water. Therefore, drowning can occur in relatively shallow water, and a person can drown without being completely underwater. Events that cause drowning might not be related to a person's swimming ability and can happen at any time. There is often the misperception that good swimmers will not drown. This is simply not true. Seizures in the water are the most frequent event that can lead to drowning for people of all ages. Other events that can lead to drowning include hyperventilating before holding the breath for underwater swimming, heart attack, stroke, and traumatic injury. Use of alcohol or drugs can be a causative factor if it affects a person's judgment or level of consciousness. Hypothermia can affect people's motor functions and level of consciousness, which can affect their ability to swim or help themselves. Less common events such as suicide, intentional injury, child abuse, and homicide can also be associated with drowning deaths.

You can interrupt the drowning process at any time by bringing a submerged person back to the surface so that he or she can breathe. The less time the person is submerged, the better the chances that the drowning person will survive, and survive without brain or organ damage.

The RID Factor

Each year, drownings occur in swimming pools with lifeguards on duty. The first question people usually ask is "How could this happen?" In many cases, the drownings were the result of medical conditions or environmental factors. However, in some instances, the lifeguards didn't recognize that a person was drowning or there were no visible symptoms to recognize.

Frank Pia, a former chief lifeguard in Orchard Beach, New York, was the first to analyze distressed or drowning swimmers' behaviors. After analyzing film of hundreds of distressed and drowning swimmers in real situations, Pia recognized three factors that contribute to a lifeguard's inability to respond to a drowning victim. He identified these as the RID factor and defined them in an article, "The RID Factor As a Cause of Drowning." The following are the three factors:

- **R**ecognition. The lifeguard did not recognize that a person was in distress or drowning because the victim did not splash or cry for help; the victim's struggle was silent and lasted just 20 to 60 seconds.
- **I**ntrusion. The lifeguard did not watch patrons closely because other tasks, such as maintenance or cleaning, intruded on his or her ability to scan.
- **D**istraction. The lifeguard was distracted because she or he was bored or engaged in conversation with peers or patrons.

Modified from F. Pia, 1984.

As you go through this training course, you will learn how to counter the RID factor by focusing on the most important aspects of lifeguarding. You will also learn how to execute. This means performing well to get the job done and obtain results. The ability to follow through with execution fills the gap between knowledge and performance. Even if you know all the facts about lifeguarding and can perform certain lifeguarding skills, you must also be able to combine your knowledge and skill in real-life situations. Execution does not happen by itself. You must make a conscious effort to be responsible for your actions and to follow best practices.

Your Work Environment

The situations in which you may find yourself lifeguarding are diverse. Places that employ lifeguards include the following:

Municipal park and recreation department

State or national park

Pool management company

Outdoor waterpark

Indoor waterpark

Neighborhood or homeowners association

School or university

Military base

Hospital rehabilitation center

Fitness and health club

Country club

Hotel or resort

Condominium or apartment complex

Nonprofit organization such as the YMCA or Jewish Community Center (JCC)

Camp

Outdoor education agency

Adventure travel company

Wilderness-based youth program

Backcountry guide service

Each of these work environments is different and has different features. Aquatic facilities may be outdoors or indoors and have treated water or freshwater. Features may include moving water, still water, slides, rocks, beaches, play structures, and zero-depth entry.

Each work environment also offers a variety of activities, such as water aerobics, swim lessons, scuba, synchronized swimming, water polo, triathlon swimming competitions, sailing, and use of personal watercraft. Attendance levels will also vary. Some aquatic facilities host thousands of patrons per day, while others see only an occasional swimmer.

However, two things will remain constant wherever you go:

1. Your *focus* on making sure patrons can remain above water so that they can breathe

2. Your commitment to *execution* and using the proven methods known as best practices

Because each work environment is unique, you must obtain additional training that is specific to your workplace. Site-specific training will include the facility's operational policy and emergency procedures and the use and care of rescue equipment.

If you can focus and execute, you will have an impact on people's lives that is greater than you may ever know. There are not many jobs where you can, through simple intervention, save lives. For each person you affect, the result is immeasurable.

The Starfish Story

Early one morning, while walking along the ocean shore, a man came upon a stretch of beach covered with hundreds of starfish. Also on the beach was a young woman. The man watched as she picked up starfish one at a time and put them gently back into the waves. "What are you doing?" he asked. The woman explained, "The tide has washed the starfish onto the beach, and they cannot return to the sea by themselves. They are in danger of dying from the relentless sun beating down." The man gazed in wonder as she again and again moved a starfish from the sand into the water. At last he spoke: "There are too many! How can you think that what you are doing can possibly make a difference?" Once again she bent down and picked up another starfish. As the starfish was released into the cool safety of the water, she simply replied, "It made a difference to that one."

Author unknown

StarGuard Performance Goals

Apply your knowledge of events that can cause drowning and knowledge of the RID factor when you lifeguard.

StarGuard Best Practices

- Focus: Watch to see that patrons' heads remain above water, or that they return to the surface after submerging, so that they can breathe.
- Execute: Save lives by understanding the importance of what you do and why you do it.

Managing Aquatic Risks

Aquatic risk management includes all of the components that are in place at an aquatic facility to help reduce the chance that someone will become ill or injured or will drown. As a lifeguard, you are part of the risk management system, so this chapter will explain the components as described in the Starfish Risk Management Model and how they relate to you. This includes knowing preventive strategies and those factors that contribute to drownings, illnesses, and injuries as well as the importance of having an emergency action plan (EAP).

Starfish Risk Management Model

The Starfish Risk Management Model has five components:

   1. Prevention strategy. This includes all of the "behind the scenes" components in place to reduce the risk of patrons becoming ill or injured or drowning.

   2. Surveillance. Watching patrons, monitoring their behavior, and recognizing emergencies play a large role in reducing risk.

   3. Emergency care. If an illness, injury, or drowning occurs, you must have a plan and be prepared to provide emergency care, whether the person is conscious or unconscious.

   4. Aquatic rescue. During a rescue, you must understand what needs to be accomplished and use best practices to manage the emergency.

   5. Professionalism and personal safety. Your behavior while you perform the lifeguarding duties described in the previous four components determines your

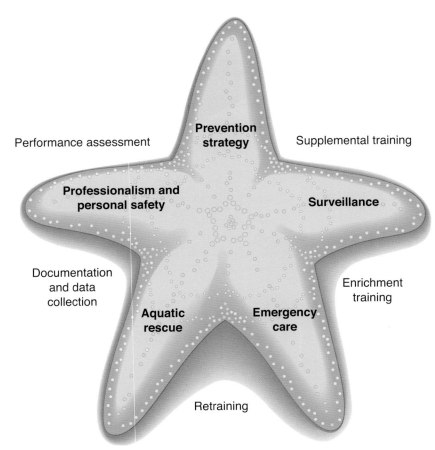

Performance assessment

Prevention strategy

Supplemental training

Professionalism and personal safety

Surveillance

Documentation and data collection

Aquatic rescue

Emergency care

Enrichment training

Retraining

Starfish risk management model.

professional image. You should also consider your own safety as a priority when you are on the job.

Each component of the risk management model is separate but dependent on the others—just like the appendages of a starfish. If any part is weak or missing, your ability to minimize overall risk will be reduced.

Let's look more closely at a realistic concept of prevention and how it relates to your job as a lifeguard.

Prevention Strategy

Lifeguard training, education, and standards have changed significantly in the last several years. Gone are the days when a coach, teacher, or beach attendant could be expected to serve as a lifeguard while performing other duties. Today, the role of a lifeguard is extremely proactive, which involves constantly and exclusively watching the water and the patrons in it. In the past, the role of a lifeguard was more reactive, which meant being available to make a rescue when notified that someone was in trouble.

Although prevention is at the heart of your job, you shouldn't take it to mean that if a patron suffers an injury, or even drowns, that it was your fault because you didn't prevent the event. Despite your best reasonable efforts, accidents happen. If you see dangerous or risky behavior, you can intervene and reduce the chance of an accident, but you can't watch everyone all the time. You also can't prevent accidents if patrons choose to disregard your warnings or don't use common sense, such as when caregivers leave children unattended, nonswimmers enter the water without a life jacket, or people dive into shallow water where "No Diving" signs are posted. In these instances, patron actions can cause an emergency situation.

Rather than thinking that prevention is solely the job of the lifeguard, you and the facility managers where you work should focus on your mutual responsibility for implementing prevention strategies. Having a strategy implies that several layers of protection are in place, all designed to help reduce the chance of injury, illness, or drowning. Patrons should share in this responsibility as well.

Layers of Protection

The layers of protection that make up a prevention strategy will vary, based on the specific risks present, but they include the following:

- Design (safety) features. The way a facility is designed (e.g., layout and barriers) and the type of materials used (e.g., non-slip flooring) can help reduce the risk of injury and control access.

- Warnings. Signs can help reduce injury by warning patrons of dangerous conditions or communicating important information.

- Rules. Rules should spell out the behavior expected at all times of everyone at a facility and should be posted in a visible location. Examples of two common rules include no running and no diving in shallow water.

- Policy and procedure. Policy helps guide decisions, and is a rule for specific circumstances that may not apply to all users. Well-designed policy that is strictly enforced can be one of the most effective layers of protection. Examples of policies include defining the age at which children may enter a facility unattended, identifying the types of flotation devices allowed, restricting nonswimmers to certain areas, requiring the use of life jackets, and restricting the use of play features to patrons of certain heights. Procedures describe actions to be taken in specific circumstances, including responding to emergencies. Procedures provide the framework for managing incidents and handling problems.

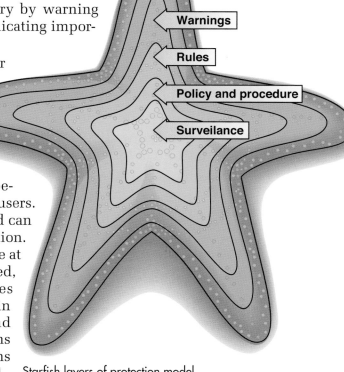

Starfish layers of protection model.

- Surveillance. The location and number of lifeguards and the scanning strategies expected of the lifeguards are a significant layer of protection.

- Inspections and performance audits. Regular and frequent inspections can either verify that the pool area, mechanical room, locker rooms, common areas, and facility exterior are in good repair or identify problems that need to be fixed. Performance audits can verify whether lifeguards provide adequate surveillance, perform in a professional manner, and can manage an emergency, or identify that remediation is necessary. A performance audit usually consists of observing and evaluating a lifeguard while he or she is on duty, and then conducting and evaluating a rescue scenario.

Because policy can be such an effective layer of protection, let's look at the reasons behind some of the policies that may be present at the facility where you work. Most policy has been developed to try to control dangerous patron behavior. You need to understand what kinds of behaviors can contribute to accidents, so you understand how enforcing a policy can help to reduce risk.

High-Risk Behaviors and Policies to Control Them

Many known factors contribute to injuries, drownings, and illnesses in an aquatic environment. The following are the most common patron behaviors that contribute to injury at an aquatic facility:

- Running
- Horseplay
- Collision with another patron
- Diving into shallow water
- Striking the wall, diving board, or other equipment

The following are the most common patron behaviors that contribute to drowning:

- Lack of adult supervision for children and unsupervised group outings
- Breath-holding contests
- Bobbing or wading into deeper water, then being unable to lift the mouth or nose out of the water or choking on water
- Being a nonswimmer in deep water without a life jacket
- Slipping off a flotation device such as a noodle or raft
- Having a seizure, heart attack, or other medical condition while in the water
- Not resting and becoming exhausted
- Being under the influence of alcohol or drugs

Finally, the following are the most common patron behaviors that can contribute to recreational water illness:

- Swallowing recreational water (treated water in pools, spas, waterparks, or spray parks)
- Swallowing freshwater that contains contaminants such as wildlife feces, fertilizer runoff, or pesticides
- Fecal accidents in the water
- Diaper changing near recreational water

The following policies, which should be modified for site-specific circumstances, can help prevent injury, illness, and drowning by reducing the likelihood of high-risk patron behaviors:

- Your facility should restrict the use of starting blocks to those diving under the direct supervision of an instructor or coach. When not it use, mark starting blocks with warning signs or put covers on them to prevent patrons from having access.
- Restrict all headfirst entries (dives) from the side, starting blocks, or diving boards to those with a hands above the head body position. Restrict novice divers from performing any technique that takes them back toward the board, side, or block during the dive.
- Lifeguards are not baby-sitters, and they can't watch all children at all times. So that parents and guardians do not leave children unattended, your facility should have a policy that requires all children under a certain age to be accompanied by a responsible person of a certain age (required ages will vary from facility to facility). An even stronger policy requires all preschool children or nonswimmers to be

directly supervised, within touching distance, by a responsible adult. Posting signs that clearly state the responsibility of the parent or caregiver and how this may relate to the responsibility of the lifeguard can help you enforce a supervision policy.

• Events such as day-camp trips, group outings, or parties held at an aquatic facility can present supervision problems and create additional risk. Often group leaders or party hosts inappropriately view the trip to the pool as a chance to relax and turn over responsibility to the lifeguards. They also may be unaware of the swimming ability of the children in attendance and not understand the need to make sure nonswimmers wear life jackets. The energy level of the participants is often high, and peer pressure can encourage children to try activities that would not be allowed under parental supervision. The group leaders or party hosts should understand that they are responsible for the direct supervision of the participants and should be required to maintain a reasonable leader-to-participant ratio. A badge or vest that identifies the adults with the group as "child watchers" can help you know who the group leaders are, and communicate a sense of responsibility to those assigned the identification. Conducting a group orientation before the participants enter the water helps reduce the risk during these events. The orientation should include the following:

  ○ Identifying group leaders
  ○ Defining the responsibilities of the leaders
  ○ Identifying the deep and shallow areas of the facility
  ○ Explaining the rules and policies
  ○ Locating life jackets, if available
  ○ Explaining restrictions and supervision requirements for nonswimmers
  ○ Identifying nonswimmers

• A policy that prohibits breath-holding contests, underwater swimming contests, and unsupervised hypoxic training drills (breath holding while swimming) can help reduce the risk of swimmers passing out while underwater due to lack of oxygen. Hypoxic training should be allowed only when conducted under the supervision of a certified coach who assumes responsibility for his or her swimmers and follows the guidelines of his or her certifying agency.

• "Deep water" is relative to the height of a swimmer and can be considered anything above chest level for that person. A policy that requires nonswimmers to stay in waist-deep water can reduce the risk of drowning. Placing buoyed ropes across areas to define a depth change or using buoyed ropes to enclose areas of specific depths can help keep nonswimmers and children in shallow water. A policy that requires nonswimmers or weak swimmers to wear a U.S. Coast Guard–approved

life jacket or swimming flotation suit can reduce the risk of drowning, because the life jacket will keep the person wearing it on the surface.

- A policy that restricts use of flotation devices (such as noodles, rafts, and float toys) to certain activities or areas helps reduce the risk of drowning due to a nonswimmer or weak swimmer falling off a device. Restricting the use of large float toys also helps to keep your underwater view clear.

- A policy that requests physician approval in writing before allowing patrons to participate in certain activities, such as exercise classes, may reduce the risk of a medical emergency happening at your facility.

- A policy that requires a rest break by clearing the water on a prescribed schedule can help reduce the risk of swimmers, particularly children, becoming overtired.

- A policy that prohibits alcohol and drug use in the facility and having a procedure for evicting patrons suspected of being intoxicated or using drugs can help reduce the risk of impaired swimmers being in the water.

Policies that can help prevent waterborne illnesses include the following:

- A policy that asks parents to instruct children not to swallow or drink water in which they swim or play. Your facility's procedures to regularly test the level of sanitizing chemicals in the pool or contaminants in freshwater should help reduce the amount and risk of disease-causing germs in the water.

- A policy that requires the use of swim diapers by anyone who does not have bowel control and prohibits changing diapers on the pool deck.

The job of a lifeguard requires a duty to act in the event of an emergency. If, despite the presence of prevention strategies, an emergency should occur, you then become a responder. Before you can respond appropriately to an emergency, a plan must be in place so that you know what actions to take. Your facility's emergency action plan is the blueprint that you will follow.

Emergency Action Plans

The responsibility for the safety and well-being of patrons or program participants at an aquatic facility is often spread among several people. Each person will play an important role in the event of an aquatic emergency. What would your role be in the event of an aquatic emergency? The answer depends on many factors, including your training,

Conducting Swim Skill Tests

If a policy at your aquatic facility allows only swimmers with demonstrated swimming skills to use certain areas or enroll in certain programs, you must have a way of determining skill level. For example, the policy may state that "only people who can swim the width of the pool unassisted may use the diving boards " or "children must be able to swim 25 yards (or 23 meters) without stopping before enrolling in the swim team program." Swim skill tests will determine whether someone can meet the requirements. It will not be practical to conduct swim skill tests on every patron who enters an aquatic facility, but a testing method should be in place to screen users of a particular area, attraction, or activity as needed.

When conducting a swim test, you place a person with unknown and untested skill in a high-risk situation. Therefore, you must minimize the risk and provide constant and dedicated attention to the swim test participant. You can accomplish this by doing the following:

- Be aware that a person's assessment of his or her swimming ability may not be accurate.
- Test in water no more than waist deep for the participant.
- Test along a wall or dock if possible, and walk along the edge to watch the swimmer. Allow only feetfirst entry during the test—no diving.
- Test no more than two swimmers at a time, except when testing swimmers of known skill for endurance (completing a distance swim of a predetermined length).
- Make sure rescue equipment is ready.
- Keep a written record of all swim skill evaluations that you conduct. Include the date, time, swimmer's name, and age. Detail which skills were evaluated, including the distance and time (e.g., swim 30 feet or 9 meters, tread water for one minute). Indicate the skill assessment outcome, such as passed/failed or satisfactory/unsatisfactory, according to the criteria set up at your facility.

government regulations, local guidelines, and the decisions that the managers of your facility have made.

An emergency action plan (EAP) is a written document detailing *who* does *what* and *when* in the event of an aquatic emergency. An EAP should be

- posted in key areas for quick reference;
- simple and easy to follow;
- practiced regularly;
- designed to include everyone who will respond; and
- developed for different types of emergencies, not only drownings but also other types of dangers such as severe weather or fire.

Some of the duties to be defined for an emergency at your facility may include, depending on the emergency, responsibilities such as the following:

- Calling EMS
- Signaling for equipment and help

- Maintaining surveillance
- Removing or controlling dangerous conditions, for example shutting off gas and electricity or neutralizing chemicals
- Evacuating patrons
- Bringing equipment to the scene
- Attending to the victim and providing care
- Meeting EMS personnel, leading them to the scene, and unlocking gates or doors, as necessary
- Notifying parents or relatives
- Obtaining and securing the victim's personal belongings
- Obtaining witness statements
- Writing reports
- Notifying supervisors
- Serving as a spokesperson and providing information to the media

The chart on page 17 is an example of an emergency action plan for an unconscious drowning victim. This is an example only; you must follow the EAP specifically designed for the facility where you work.

StarGuard Performance Goal

Understand the Starfish layers of protection model and seek to develop mutual responsibility between you, your facility, and patrons for following prevention strategies.

StarGuard Best Practices

- Enforce your facility's rules and policy the same way each time.
- Practice and execute site-specific emergency action plans for various emergencies.

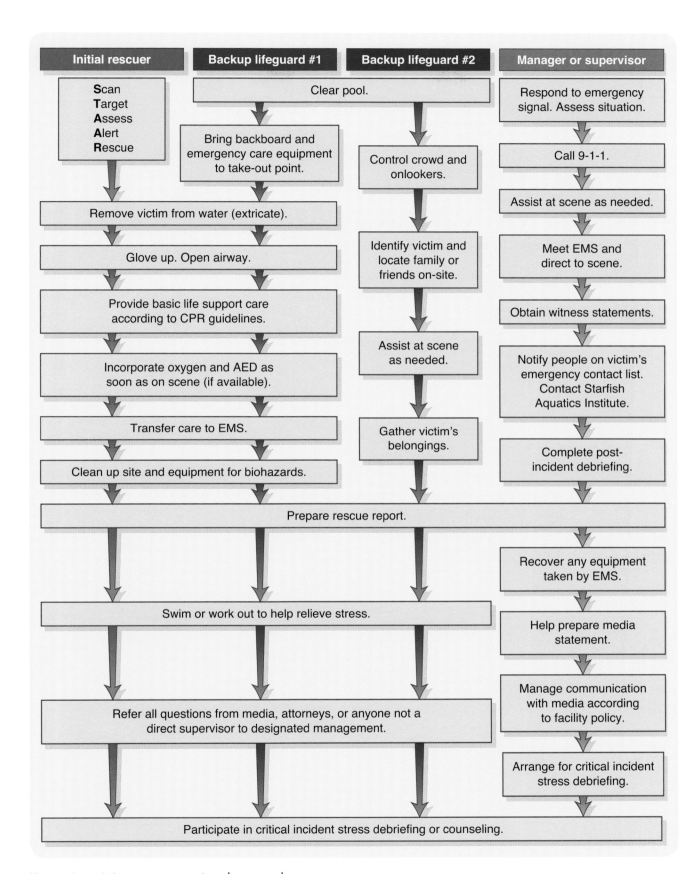

Initial rescuer	Backup lifeguard #1	Backup lifeguard #2	Manager or supervisor

Scan
Target
Assess
Alert
Rescue

Clear pool.

Respond to emergency signal. Assess situation.

Bring backboard and emergency care equipment to take-out point.

Control crowd and onlookers.

Call 9-1-1.

Remove victim from water (extricate).

Assist at scene as needed.

Glove up. Open airway.

Identify victim and locate family or friends on-site.

Meet EMS and direct to scene.

Provide basic life support care according to CPR guidelines.

Obtain witness statements.

Assist at scene as needed.

Incorporate oxygen and AED as soon as on scene (if available).

Notify people on victim's emergency contact list. Contact Starfish Aquatics Institute.

Transfer care to EMS.

Gather victim's belongings.

Clean up site and equipment for biohazards.

Complete post-incident debriefing.

Prepare rescue report.

Recover any equipment taken by EMS.

Swim or work out to help relieve stress.

Help prepare media statement.

Manage communication with media according to facility policy.

Refer all questions from media, attorneys, or anyone not a direct supervisor to designated management.

Arrange for critical incident stress debriefing.

Participate in critical incident stress debriefing or counseling.

Unconscious victim emergency action plan example.

Preventing Bloodborne and Recreational Water Illness

One of the unpleasant but necessary parts of your job is to clean up vomit or fecal material in the water and surrounding areas. Do this quickly and correctly to avoid spreading disease to patrons or yourself. You also may have contact with blood and bodily fluids when providing first aid, although you should use protective equipment to avoid direct contact with these substances.

This chapter explains how to prevent exposure to potentially disease-causing pathogens by using personal protection equipment and by properly cleaning up fecal matter and bodily fluids in the pool area and disinfecting the area.

Disease Transmission Through Bodily Substances

Most bodily substances, especially blood, vomit, and fecal matter can contain disease. The germs that can be transmitted through direct contact with blood and bodily fluids are called bloodborne pathogens, and they include HIV and hepatitis B (HBV) among others. Vomit may contain noroviruses (also known as Norwalk-like viruses). Fecal matter can contain deadly disease-causing bacteria such as E. coli and parasites such as giardia and cryptosporidium (also known as crypto) as well as the hepatitis A virus.

You can prevent transmission of each of these viruses, bacteria, and parasites by isolating yourself and others from contact by disinfecting the water and surrounding surfaces to kill the germs. The first step in isolating a bodily substance is to consider everything to be infected and to protect yourself from becoming exposed through the use of protective equipment.

Universal Precautions and Personal Protection Equipment

Because you cannot look at a bodily substance and know if it is infected, assume that all bodily fluids and feces could contain pathogens. This approach to contact is called universal precautions. It is also sometimes referred to as standard precautions. Always use personal protection equipment (PPE) when you are at risk of exposure to any type of bodily substance. The personal protective equipment available for your use should include vinyl or latex gloves, a pocket mask or face shield, protective eyewear, and protective footwear.

Vinyl or Latex Gloves

Gloves will help protect you from pathogens that could enter your body through a break in the skin around your nails or on your hands. Gloves come in several sizes and thicknesses and should fit snugly, but not so tight that the glove will break. If you have a sensitivity or allergy to latex, you may prefer to use gloves made out of vinyl or silicone.

It is difficult to put dry gloves onto wet hands, especially when you are in a hurry. If your hands are wet, and you are near the water, it may help to fill your glove with water, then slip your wet hand into the wet glove.

Remove gloves in a way that prevents bodily fluids that might be on the gloves from coming in contact with your skin. To remove gloves, do the following:

  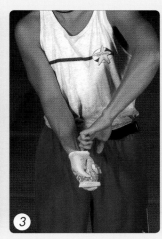 

Grasp one glove at the base of the palm, pulling it slightly away from the hand, then pull the glove up and slide the hand out so that the glove comes off inside out.	Cup the removed glove inside the palm of your gloved hand.	Slide a finger (or fingers) of your bare hand under and inside the base of the remaining glove. Pull the glove up and slide your hand out so that the glove comes off inside out, with the first glove inside.	Discard the soiled gloves in a biohazard disposal bag or container. Wash your hands immediately with warm running water and soap or with waterless antibacterial cleanser.

Barrier Masks

A barrier mask helps reduce the transfer of bodily fluids between you and the person on whom you are performing rescue breathing or CPR. Several types of barrier masks are available with features appropriate for different circumstances. Some barrier masks are referred to as pocket masks. You will learn how to apply and use a barrier mask in your CPR training, and you will need to practice with the style of barrier mask you will use at the facility where you work.

A shield-style device provides a minimal barrier and is compact enough to be carried on a keychain or in a pocket. This type of barrier is not designed for professional rescuers.

Masks designed for professional rescuers have a larger mouthpiece and a one-way valve, and they create a seal over the mouth and nose for maximum ventilation. These barrier masks may also contain a port for an oxygen tube and may come in different sizes for use on an infant, child, or adult.

If you are performing rescue breathing in the water, the one-way valve in your barrier mask should be made of all plastic without an absorbent filter. An all-plastic design prevents the filter from absorbing water that you might blow into a person's lungs.

Protective Eyewear and Footwear

In the presence of large amounts of blood or vomit, wear some type of covering for your eyes to reduce the risk of bodily fluids splashing into your eyes and entering your body. If you are already wearing sunglasses, keep them on. If you do not have on sunglasses, put on safety glasses or goggles. Whenever you are cleaning up bodily fluids, you also need to wear some type of footwear to prevent contact with your bare feet.

Once you are protected by PPE, you can clean up the bodily substances using precautions to prevent further exposure to yourself or others. These precautions include containing the area of exposure, removing the bodily substance, disinfecting the area, disposing of potentially contaminated materials, and restricting people from using potentially contaminated areas.

Cleaning Up Bodily Fluids and Fecal Matter

Your workplace should have a specific plan for how to clean up and dispose of bodily fluids or fecal matter. A cleanup procedure should consist of at least these six key components:

1. Use universal precautions and treat all bodily substances as if they contain disease-causing pathogens. Wear your personal protective equipment.

2. Contain the area of exposure. If blood or vomit is on the floor or pool deck, mark and restrict access to the area to prevent others from walking through it and becoming exposed or spreading the bodily substance. If fecal matter or vomit is in the water, scoop out as much solid material as possible to keep it from spreading and restrict access to the water.

3. Remove a liquid bodily substance by soaking it up with an absorbing material and scooping up the material into a container. Then use paper towels to absorb or pick up any remaining substance. Commercially packaged biohazard cleanup kits usually include single-use packets of absorbing material, or it is available in large containers. As an alternative, you can use high-absorbing kitty litter. Remove a solid bodily substance by scooping it up, or picking it up inside a plastic bag.

4. Disinfect the area of exposure. Pour or spray a solution of bleach (1 part bleach to 9 parts water) over the entire area and let it sit for at least 20 minutes. Wipe up the bleach solution with paper towels and allow the area to air dry. If the exposure is in the water, follow your local health department guidelines for disinfecting the water.

5. Dispose of the contaminated materials. Place the materials in a double plastic bag, being careful not to touch the outside of the bag. Tie or close the inner bag. After cleaning any utensils you used and the cleanup process is complete, remove your gloves. Place your gloves and any other soiled items in the outer plastic bag and close the bag. If the bag is not marked as biohazard, place a biohazard label on the bag. Follow your local procedures for disposing of infectious waste.

6. Restrict use of the area. Do not allow patrons access to a land-based cleanup area until the deck, ground, or floor is completely dry. If the bodily substance was in the water, do not allow patrons to go back in until your facility has met the local health department regulations for closure.

If you come in direct contact with bodily fluids and were not using personal protection equipment, consider yourself to be "exposed." Follow your employer's exposure control plan, which may include blood testing and follow-up by health care professionals. Be sure to document on the incident report provided by your facility any exposure to yourself and others, including bystanders.

If vomit or fecal matter gets into the water, there is a slight possibility that germs may remain long enough, before being killed by the sanitizing agent, for a patron to become ill by swallowing contaminated water. Although incidents of transmitting serious disease in this manner are rare, you must understand how the risk for transmitting these diseases can be reduced.

Recreational Water Illness

A recreational water site is anywhere that people enter the water such as a pool, waterpark, hot tub/spa, lake, river, or ocean. When germs contaminate recreational water they can cause recreational water illness (RWI). Examples of germs that cause RWIs include E. coli (ee-CO-lye), giardia (gee-ARE-dee-uh), crypto (KRIP-toe; short for cryptosporidium), and shigella (shi-GE-luh). These germs, which may be a bacteria, virus, or microscopic parasite, generally enter the water through loose or liquid stools or vomit. Germs that may be present in blood don't survive in chlorinated water and do not pose a threat. Loose or liquid stools (diarrhea) spread readily and are more likely to be infected with bacteria. Viruses are more likely to be present in vomit when the full contents of the stomach have been emptied, which may indicate that a person is sick. Germs are less likely to be present in a small amount of vomit, which is a common occurrence when a child swallows too much water, especially right after eating.

Chlorine kills germs that can contaminate water, but the chlorine does not work immediately on some types of pathogens. For example, in water treated with chlorine at levels that meet health department standards, E. coli can live for less than one minute, and some viruses will live for about 16 minutes. Parasites can be harder to kill. Giardia survives about 45 minutes, and cryptosporidium can survive for days. Patrons get exposed to RWI's by swallowing recreational water or coming in contact with bodily substances that may be present around the recreational area. Patrons that are most at risk for getting very sick from an RWI include children, pregnant women, and those that have an immune system deficiency caused by HIV, chemotherapy, or other conditions. Whenever people swim, a small amount of water will always be ingested. This is why your local or state regulatory agency will determine the guidelines for how long your aquatic facility may have to be closed in the event of vomit or fecal matter in the pool. The amount of time is usually based on the chemical levels in the water, the rate of water turnover through the filters, and whether the contaminant was fecal matter, diarrhea, or vomit. Table 3.1 provides general guidelines for cleaning up bodily fluids and fecal matter.

The most effective way to control exposure to recreational water illnesses is to keep water from becoming contaminated. Educating patrons about how to avoid contaminating the water is the first step. Your employer should post signs and distribute information for patrons about how to reduce the spread of recreational water illness. The Centers for Disease Control and Prevention (CDC), has established a list of healthy swimming behaviors for protection against RWIs that should be included as the foundation to educate patrons:

- PLEASE do not swim when you have diarrhea. This is especially important for kids in diapers.
- PLEASE do not swallow the pool water.
- PLEASE practice good hygiene. Take a shower before swimming and wash your hands after using the toilet or changing diapers.
- PLEASE take your kids on bathroom breaks or check diapers often.

Table 3.1 Cleaning Up Blood, Vomit, and Fecal Accidents in Chlorinated Recreational Water

	Vomit, blood, solid fecal	Vomit (full stomach contents)	Solid fecal (formed stool)	Diarrhea
Location	Deck or solid surface	In water	In water	In water
Containment	Mark off area. Apply absorbing agent to liquid.	Clear pool.	Clear pool.	Clear pool.
Precautions	Wear latex or vinyl disposable gloves. Wear shoes. Wash hands with soap and water when cleanup is completed.			
Removal	Scoop or pick up. Wipe up with paper towels; place in plastic garbage bag.	Use net or scoop to remove as much as possible; place in plastic garbage bag.	Use net or scoop to remove fecal matter from pool without breaking it apart; place in plastic garbage bag.	Use net or scoop to remove as much as possible; place in plastic garbage bag.
Disinfection	Soak area with bleach solution* or commercial disinfectant for 20 mins. Use bleach or disinfectant to wash nondisposable cleaning tools.	Adjust water chemistry to a minimum 2.0 ppm chlorine and 7.2-7.5 pH (if not already within these readings). Maintain levels for at least 25 mins. If chlorine level is at 3.0 ppm, maintain for 19 mins. Soak net or scoop in pool water during this time to disinfect.		Adjust water chemistry to a minimum of 10 ppm chlorine and 7.2-7.5 pH. Maintain levels for 16 hrs. Backwash filter (sending water to waste).
Disposal	Place the materials in a double plastic bag, being careful not to touch the outside of the bag. Tie or close the inner bag. After cleaning any utensils you used and the cleanup process is complete, remove your gloves. Place your gloves in the outer plastic bag and close the bag. Tie the bag and tag it with a biohazard label (if available). Place in trash or dispose of according to your local regulations.			
Restriction	Immediate area: 20 mins	Entire pool and any others that share the same filter: 19-25 mins depending on chlorine level		Entire pool and any others that share the same filter: 16 hrs at 10 ppm chlorine, 8 hrs at 20 ppm chlorine

*Bleach solution: 1 part bleach to 9 parts water

This information is based on the recommendations of the Centers for Disease Control and Prevention (CDC), but it does not replace existing guidelines from your local or state regulatory agency.

- PLEASE change diapers in a bathroom and not at poolside.
- PLEASE wash your child (especially the rear end) thoroughly with soap and water before swimming.

This information is available in poster form at www.cdc.gov/healthyswimming.

Never knowingly allow patrons to enter a filtered body of water that does not have enough sanitizing chemicals to kill pathogens and bacteria or a fresh body of water that has a high bacteria count. Treated water should be tested several times per day using a test kit designed for measuring the chlorine level in the water. The regulations of your local health department will determine how often during a day these tests must be conducted. If you are responsible for testing water, adding chemicals to the water, or backwashing to clean the pool filters, you must obtain additional site-specific training in pool operation and chemical handling safety procedures.

A common testing schedule for freshwater is weekly or more frequently if required by your local health department regulations or if bacteria levels are above a certain point. The usual procedure is to obtain a water sample in a sterilized container and take it to a laboratory approved by your local health department for testing.

StarGuard Performance Goal

Protect yourself and patrons from contact with bodily substances. Consider all bodily substances as contaminated and educate patrons on how to prevent recreational water illnesses.

StarGuard Best Practices

- Use personal protective equipment.
- Clean up bodily substances according to your health department or Center for Disease Control (CDC) guidelines.
- Practice putting on and removing latex gloves, especially when your hands are wet.
- Teach patrons how to prevent recreational water illness; use resources from the CDC.
- Test water frequently to make sure sanitation is adequate.

Preventing Injuries

Three effective ways to minimize the risk of injuries are to eliminate or reduce known hazards, be prepared for environmental hazards such as weather, and enforce rules that protect patrons. The first part of this chapter shows you how to identify hazards in and around an aquatic facility and provides tips for electrical safety and for evacuation in case of severe weather. The second part of this chapter presents strategies to help you identify potentially dangerous or suspicious behavior and communicate with patrons, including large crowds, to effectively enforce rules and policy.

Inspections and Hazard Identification

Part of your job as a lifeguard is to watch for hazards or conditions at your facility that might threaten patrons' safety. This is true whether you are working at an indoor or outdoor facility. Examples of indoor hazards may include the following:

Equipment Defects

Broken or nonfunctioning equipment

Loose bolts

Rust on support beams

Loose railings or handrails

Loose stairs or footholds

Broken grates

Cracked or broken lane-line floats
Broken fixtures
Sharp edges or protrusions
Leaks
Cracks
Exposed wires or overloaded plugs

Fall-Causing Hazards

Loose carpet
Debris
Standing water
Obstructions
Inadequate lighting

Security Risks

Damaged locks
Doors that do not latch or open properly
Suspicious persons

Air, Water, or Chemical Hazards

Poor air or water quality
Unsanitary conditions
Improperly stored chemicals or cleaning products

Missing Items

Missing signs or markings
Missing equipment or supplies

Additional hazards at outdoor and waterfront areas may include the following:

Wildlife
Extreme temperatures
Weather conditions

Glare
Currents, riptides, or undertows
Submerged rocks or stumps
Turbid (cloudy or dark) water
Sharp objects or debris
Holes or drop-offs
Falling limbs or trees
Obstructions
Watercraft
Unstable docks or piers
Rotting or broken pier slats
Changing water levels under platforms
Missing or inadequate buoy line to mark swim area

Your employer should have a system for frequently inspecting the areas used by patrons. This is especially important for waterfront areas where natural hazards may form over time or debris may wash up on the shore. If you find a hazard that can't be immediately removed or fixed, you must limit access to the area and point out the dangerous condition to patrons. When possible, post warning signs or use barricades to keep people out of the hazardous area. Report hazards to your supervisor, or follow the procedure at your facility.

In addition to the physical hazards in an aquatic facility, electricity can pose a risk. Electricity is present in the wiring used to power the pool pumps, lights, and other systems as well as in the outlets used for equipment. Electricity can also be present in the form of lightning, so you should understand the strategies for electrical safety and how to monitor thunderstorms.

Electrical Safety

Water and electricity can create a deadly mix. Take these precautions to prevent electrical shock:

- Keep electrical devices away from the water's edge.
- Elevate cords or cover cords on the ground with a mat or tape to prevent tripping.
- Know where the main power switch is for your facility; shut off power in the event of an injury from electrical shock. If the power cannot be turned off, use something that does not conduct electricity, such as wood, to remove the source of voltage from contact with the victim.

Monitoring Severe Weather Conditions

To reduce the risk of injury from severe weather, closely monitor weather conditions and be prepared to quickly direct swimmers out of the water and direct patrons out of the surrounding area. Here are ways to monitor the weather:

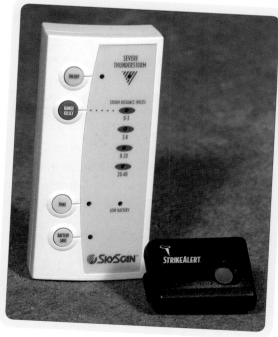

- Emergency weather radios are inexpensive and provide warning signals when the National Weather Service issues severe weather statements.
- Live satellite and radar images and local forecasts are available on the Weather Channel and on weather information Web sites.
- Lightning detectors provide an early warning of approaching lightning. These devices measure the lightning strike distance, track the storm direction, and sound an alert when lightning is within a dangerous range. Lightning sensors, which are shown in this photo, come in two forms: a device permanently mounted to a pole attached to a building or portable devices that can be clipped to a belt or carried.

Be familiar with weather conditions unique to your location. Knowledge of local weather patterns, such as where storms usually form and the direction they take, can be useful in making safety decisions. To determine if a storm is approaching your location, do the following:

- Watch the movement of the clouds; a storm may move in a different direction than the wind at ground level.
- Note abrupt changes in wind direction and speed as well as a sudden drop in temperature; both can be signs that you are in the path of a storm.

Emergency action plans (EAP) are needed for severe weather as well as for aquatic emergencies. Learn the steps in your facility's severe weather emergency action plan. The EAP should detail evacuation procedures for a tornado warning and lightning-generating storms.

If your facility does not have a lightning detector, instruct swimmers to exit the water and patrons to leave the surrounding area whenever you see lightning or hear thunder. Lightning can develop a great distance ahead of a storm cloud and may appear to come out of clear blue sky. Consider yourself in striking distance whenever you can hear thunder from an approaching storm.

Keep swimmers out of the water until a passing storm is at least 10 miles (16 kilometers) away. In most instances, the storm has moved on and threat is minimal when 30 minutes have passed since the last lightning or thunder. You can use the "flash-bang" rule of thumb to monitor how quickly the storm is moving toward you. When you see lightning flash, count the seconds until you hear the thunder. For every five seconds you count, the electrical storm is 1 mile (1.6 kilometers) away. Here is an example:

Every 5 seconds between lightning and thunder =
1 mile (1.6 kilometers) to storm

10 seconds between lightning and thunder =
2 miles (3.2 kilometers) to storm

If an electrical storm approaches and you are outdoors, direct patrons out of the water and to the closest safe location. A primary safe location is any building that people normally or frequently occupy. A secondary safe location could be any vehicle with a hard metal roof and rolled-up windows. If an electrical storm approaches and you are at an indoor aquatic facility, instruct patrons to exit the water. Follow the EAP for severe weather at your facility. When patrons are out of the water and located in a primary shelter, prohibit using land-line telephones, taking a shower, and touching surfaces exposed to the outside, such as metal doors, windows, electrical wiring, cable, and plumbing. Electricity can travel indoors through these paths and could cause injury to persons in these situations.

The most dangerous hazard in an aquatic facility is the behavior of the people who use the facility. Rules are made to help control dangerous behavior and actions. Because enforcing the rules will be an important part of your job, let's explore some ways to effectively communicate the rules to patrons.

Rules and Policy Enforcement

First, you need to know the rules at your facility and the reason for each rule. Make sure that you understand each rule and that your fellow lifeguards understand it in the same way. Then, you need to effectively enforce the rules. You will have the most success getting patrons to follow the rules at your facility if you take a positive, professional approach. To be effective when enforcing a rule, follow these steps:

1. Signal to get a patron's attention, using the method designated at your facility. If your facility is crowded and noisy, you may need to blow a whistle or speak into a megaphone to attract attention; if it is less crowded, you may be able to speak directly to the patron more discreetly.

2. Use verbal or nonverbal communication to indicate to a patron that what he or she is doing is not acceptable. If the person does not understand or does not respond, then ask the person to come talk to you.

3. Once the patron comes to you, keep watching the water and explain to the patron that you are required to keep your attention on the swimmers in the water while you are talking. That way the patron won't mistake your lack of eye contract for a lack of respect or poor customer service.

4. Be courteous and positive when you talk to the patron. Use phrases such as "Please walk" instead of "Don't run," or "We only allow plastic bottles" instead of "You can't have glass in here." Briefly explain that the reason for a rule is to keep patrons safe, not to restrict their fun or enjoyment.

5. Use a "sandwich approach" when discussing a rule or policy infraction. Say something positive to the patron, state what you want the patron to do, and then say something positive again. Here's an example: "Ma'am, we're glad you are enjoying our pool today with your children. I want you to be aware that we have a policy that all small children need to be within arm's reach of an adult when they are in the water, so please stay in the water with your children. Thank you, we want everyone to be safe while having fun. "

Whenever you are guarding, be consistent; enforce the same rule or policy the same way for everyone, each time. If a patron refuses to comply with a rule or policy, notify your supervisor, using the communication system in place at your facility.

Watching for Threatening Behaviors

Besides knowing how to reduce hazards and enforce rules, you also must watch for behaviors that might be harmful to others. Aquatic facilities are usually open to the general public and although the aquatic playground setting attracts people who want to enjoy themselves, it can also attract people with other intentions. For example, child predators go where children go. The threat of gang violence, terrorism, sexual predation, and other antisocial acts is present in any public location that attracts large crowds. If you notice suspicious behavior or activity, report it immediately to your supervisor. This behavior may include the following:

- Leaving unidentified packages unattended and where they should not be left
- Videotaping children he or she appears not to know
- Making frequent physical contact, especially in the water, with children he or she appears not to know
- Using the locker rooms and changing rooms frequently or for prolonged amounts of time
- A male loitering or interacting with children without appearing to have any of his own
- Entering the locker room or changing room of the opposite sex
- Entering a facility not dressed in swimwear
- Congregating outside the fence
- Talking about or showing off a weapon
- Indecent exposure
- Sexual activity, gestures, intimate contact, or harrasment

If you encounter serious disturbances such as violence among patrons, follow your facility emergency action plan for these incidents. Any time a behavior is suspicious enough for concern, call for police assistance and have them address the situation.

Crowd Management

During crowded conditions or emergencies, your ability to manage large groups of people will be very important. You may have to deal with a crowd to communicate safety information, make emergency announcements, provide direction, control violence, or evacuate the facility.

First, get the crowd's attention and make sure that patrons can hear you. Use a microphone or megaphone if available. Then give directions in short phrases, spoken in a loud, clear voice. Repeat the announcement several times. Provide information that is accurate but simple; skip unnecessary detail or explanation. An example of poor communication might be the following announcement: "May

I have your attention. We've just been notified by the National Weather Service that a tornado warning has been issued for Clark, Wayne, and Green counties until 7:30 P.M. A tornado has been sighted near Eldorado and is heading this way. Please get out of the water, gather your belongings, and seek shelter. If you don't have transportation, go to the locker rooms. If you have questions, see the pool manager." A better way to communicate this information would be like this: "Attention. Severe weather is approaching and a tornado warning has been issued. Please clear the pool immediately." Additional details or assistance could be provided by staff as people leave or seek shelter.

Make announcements in the language of the majority of patrons. If large groups of patrons speak other languages (more than 30 percent), make announcements in more than one language. It is also helpful if the signage at your facility is in more than one language or uses descriptive pictures to illustrate safety and emergency instructions.

StarGuard Performance Goal

Minimize the risk of injury by reducing known hazards, being prepared for environmental hazards, and enforcing rules and policies that protect patrons.

StarGuard Best Practices

- Inspect your facility frequently for hazards.
- Shut off the power in the event of an injury from electrical shock.
- Monitor severe weather conditions and know the evacuation procedures at your facility.
- Know and enforce rules and policies with a positive, sandwich approach.
- Watch for threatening or suspicious behaviors and, if observed, notify your supervisor.

PART II

Surveillance

Objectives

Knowledge	Skill	Execution
After reading part II, you should understand the following:	After hands-on and in-water practice, you should be able to perform the following:	After scenario and site-specific training you should be able to do the following:
The priority of constant, dedicated surveillance The factors that determine zone size and areas of responsibility The behavior characteristics of distress and drowning The definition of drowning The effects on the body of the drowning process How to use scanning patterns The functions of three observation skills: scan, target, assess The reasons for using the 10/20 rule, triage scanning, the 5-Minute Scanning Strategy, and a proactive rotation The role of technology in providing underwater surveillance The need to locate lifeguard chairs so that you can see the entire zone The basic functions of an emergency communication system The common emergency whistle and hand and arm signals	Scanning patterns Triage scanning 5-Minute Scanning Strategy Proactive rotation Whistle blasts Arm signals for "I need help" and "zone clear and covered"	Provide surveillance using a system of scanning and vigilance techniques Recognize distressed swimmers and drowning victims

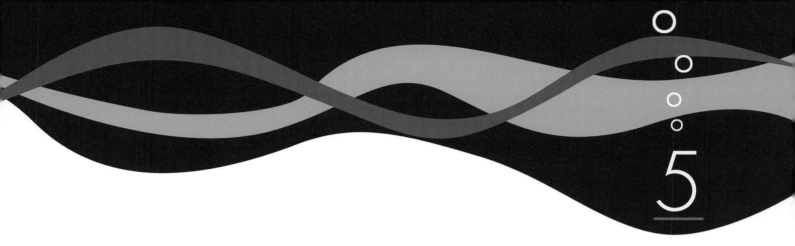

Recognizing a Drowning Victim

One of the most important skills you must develop as a lifeguard is the ability to recognize when a swimmer needs help so that you can intervene quickly. This chapter defines distress and drowning, explains the drowning process, and outlines the observational skills you will use regularly as a lifeguard.

A drowning person *does not* look like the stereotype portrayed in movies or drawings: someone frantically waving arms or shouting for help. A distressed or drowning person exhibits behaviors that are much more subtle and difficult to detect.

Distress

Generally, a person in distress is still on the surface of the water but is struggling to stay afloat. The person's mouth or nose or both are above the surface, and he or she is still able to breathe. Some behaviors that indicate that a person is in distress include the following:

- Head back and body low in the water
- Arms extended from the sides and moving up and down
- Minimal use of the legs with little support from a kick

Often, a person in distress will try to remain upright and turn to face the nearest source of assistance, for example toward a lifeguard stand, the pool wall, or shore. If this is the case, and the person is relatively close, you may be able to recognize a fearful, wide-eyed look on his or her face. However, you cannot rely only on

facial expression to indicate distress because a person may be facing away from you, or blocked from your view by other people.

If distress continues, the person's mouth and nose will sink below the surface of the water, and he or she will begin to drown. How quickly a person progresses from distress to drowning varies depending on many circumstances. A person who cannot keep his or her mouth and nose out of the water and breathe will die unless someone intervenes. The earlier the person receives help, the better the chance of keeping a distress situation from becoming a drowning.

Drowning Definitions

Until recently there was no standardized definition of drowning. This lack of consensus has made analysis of drowning studies difficult. In response to this problem, a group of international experts met in 2002 at the World Congress on Drowning to develop definitions and guidelines for reporting drowning data. The following is the universal definition of drowning that was adopted by consensus:

"Drowning is the process of experiencing respiratory impairment from submersion/immersion in liquid." According to the clarification that accompanied the definition, "The victim may live or die after the process, but regardless of the outcome, s/he has been a part of a drowning incident."

Other definitions related to drowning include the following:

- Drowning victim. A person involved in an incident in which the airway has been covered with water, preventing him or her from breathing air. A drowning victim that is rescued becomes a drowning survivor if he or she remains alive after a drowning event.

- Drowning survivor. The physical condition of a drowning survivor can vary from complete recovery to having permanent brain damage or heart damage. Most drowning survivors at facilities where lifeguards are present are rescued before becoming unconscious and recover completely at the scene. A drowning survivor who has lost consciousness may be resuscitated at the scene by lifeguards, during prehospital care by EMS, or at the hospital by emergency room physicians. The amount of permanent damage a drowning survivor has depends upon how long he or she was unconscious before being resuscitated, in addition to other factors. Many drowning survivors must be placed on a ventilator and fed through a tube. These drowning survivors live in what is called a "vegetative state" and cannot function without the aid of the machines keeping them alive.

- Drowning fatality. A person who dies as a result of a drowning incident. The death may occur at the scene or may occur later at the hospital as a result of lack of oxygen to the organs or infections such as pneumonia.

Now that you know the terminology associated with drowning, let's discuss the physiological changes that the body goes through during the drowning process.

Drowning Process

A person's first response to the drowning process is to hold his or her breath, followed shortly by a laryngospasm. A laryngospasm is a physical reaction to water droplets at the back of the throat that cause the top of the larynx (the windpipe that carries air from the mouth to the lungs) to close. At this time the victim tries to breathe but cannot and instead may swallow large amounts of water.

As the victim's blood-oxygen level falls, the laryngospasm relaxes and the victim may breathe water into the lungs. The amount inhaled is different for each person. Depending on how long the victim is submerged and the amount of water inhaled, the concentration of body fluids, especially electrolytes, can become diluted. Electrolytes are salts in the body that conduct electricity. If the electrolytes become diluted with large quantities of swallowed or inhaled water, the electrical impulses that cause the heart to beat can be interrupted and cause the heart to stop.

If the victim does not return to the surface and start breathing, either on his or her own or after being resuscitated, the heart will stop, brain damage caused by lack of oxygen will occur, organs will stop functioning, and the victim will die. The heart and brain are the organs at greatest risk for permanent damage during drowning, even if someone interrupts the drowning process and resuscitates the victim.

Two important factors to remember about drowning are that a person doesn't have to be submerged completely under the water for drowning to occur; a person can drown if his or her face is immersed in water. And the amount of time that passes before interruption of the drowning process is crucial to the victim's survival.

Immersion and Submersion

A person is drowning if the face and airway are covered with water, which can occur through either immersion or submersion. Immersion means that only the face and airway are covered with water. Submersion means that the entire body is underwater. Immersion can occur in relatively shallow water, such as a bucket, a puddle, or a few inches of water at a beachfront or zero-depth entry area.

Time Factors

You can interrupt drowning at any time during the process between initial voluntary breath holding and death. The earlier you interrupt the process, the better the victim's chances for survival without brain or organ damage.

The length of time a victim was immersed or submerged is the most important predictor of survival. Unless the water is very cold (less than 50 degrees Fahrenheit, or 10 degrees Celsius), brain damage and death generally occur three to five minutes after the person starts drowning, although this varies from person to person. Survival and recovery generally occur in victims that have been drowning for a short time and receive resuscitation and CPR at the scene. The graph on page 41 shows how the length of submersion relates to survival outcomes.

To intervene quickly in an emergency situation, you must rely on your observational skills. These include the ability to watch the water (scan), identify anything unusual (target), and determine if there is an emergency (assess the situation).

Observation Skills

To recognize distress or drowning, you must continuously perform three crucial observation skills: scan, target, and assess. To *scan* means to watch the water, using specific patterns and timing. If you notice a situation that might indicate a problem, you will *target* the person or people and look more closely. The next step is to *assess* the situation and determine your course of action. The following scenario illustrates how you would use your observation skills:

- Scan. While you are watching a crowded pool you notice a father holding a young child. He is standing in shoulder-deep water, and they are located near a gradual slope into deeper water. Neither exhibits distress symptoms. However,

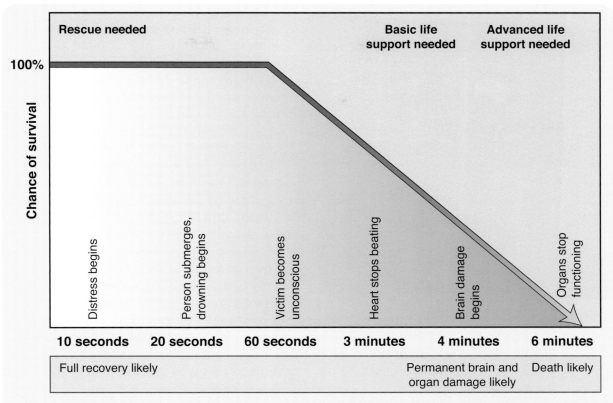

Rescue needed				**Basic life support needed**	**Advanced life support needed**	

Chance of survival

100%

Distress begins

Person submerges, drowning begins

Victim becomes unconscious

Heart stops beating

Brain damage begins

Organs stop functioning

10 seconds	20 seconds	60 seconds	3 minutes	4 minutes	6 minutes

Full recovery likely	Permanent brain and organ damage likely	Death likely

Note: This time line is a representation of general physiological responses during drowning. The individual circumstances of each drowning can cause wide variation from the times represented. Death can occur with much shorter submersion times, and survival can occur with much longer submersion times.

you notice several things about the situation that could indicate a potential problem, so you briefly target your attention to the father and child.

- Target. You target the father and child for the following reasons:
  - The father's bobbing movements are pushing him gradually back toward deeper water.
  - The child does not appear comfortable in the water.
  - The crowded conditions may prevent the father from quickly changing position and moving toward shallow water.
- Assess. You assess the situation and think about what could likely occur. Under these circumstances, the father could quickly become submerged just enough to be unable to breathe or to recover to a standing position. You decide to take action and get the attention of the father, directing him to move back toward shallower water.

Let's consider another example. A 10-year-old child is playing in water that is chest deep. He and a friend decide to move out a bit from the edge, pushing off the bottom and bobbing or maybe "wall walking" (holding on to the side) into slightly deeper water. The water is just deep enough that when the child pushes up off the bottom to get to the surface for a breath, his mouth does not clear the water. The child gulps a mouthful of water instead of air. In this situation, the child is not able to cry out for help because he is already underwater.

The child's movements may make him appear to be swimming underwater, and if you don't have a clear underwater view, you may not notice anything extraordinary during your scan. You may not be able to recognize the situation because there have been no signs of distress until the child stops moving and is unconscious. In this case, the lack of movement you notice when you scan is what causes you to target on the situation, assess it as an emergency, and begin a rescue.

Anytime you believe that a person has not moved for longer than 10 seconds, whether on the surface, faceup, or facedown, intervene and check responsiveness. Anytime you see something and are not sure what you are looking at, check to make sure it is not a drowning victim. Lifeguards who have seen a submerged drowning victim often describe what they saw as a "shadow" or a "smudge." Statements such as "I thought it was a towel on the bottom" or "It looked like the drain but it was in the wrong place" are common.

In some instances, a change in movement may cause you to target in on a situation. For example, if a patron has been swimming laps and her stroke pattern, tempo, or body position changes, this could signal distress. If a person enters deep water and begins to frantically but ineffectively move his arms to try to keep on the surface, this person could be in distress and need your immediate inter-

vention. A drowning person may still be moving and may even be near the surface but is not able to call out or wave for help. Table 5.1 provides a summary of the most common observable indications of distress or drowning.

Table 5.1 Observable Indications of Distress and Drowning

	Distress (mouth and nose are above water)	Drowning (mouth and nose are covered by water)
Can the person breathe?	Yes	No
Expression	Person may be wide-eyed with a panic-stricken look.	Expressions are usually not visible because the victim's nose and mouth are covered by water.
Condition	Conscious	Conscious or unconscious
Position	The person may face toward you or away from you. The person may be vertical, horizontal, or at an angle in the water. A conscious person's head and face may tilt back. An unconscious person may float facedown or faceup.	
Depth	Usually on the surface or alternating just underneath the surface with bobbing up to the surface for a breath	On the surface, just beneath the surface, submerged to mid-depth, or on the bottom
What this person may look like	Someone struggling to stay on the surface Someone bobbing Someone struggling to get to the side Someone struggling to grab something to stay afloat	Someone trying to stand up but can't Someone playing underwater Someone floating A shadow A smudge or blur A towel on the bottom A drain on the bottom

StarGuard Performance Goals

Use observation skills to look for behaviors that indicate distress (when a person can still breathe) or drowning (when a person's mouth and nose are covered with water).

StarGuard Best Practices

- Scan the water to look for symptoms of distress or drowning.
- Target unusual movement or lack of movement.
- Assess the situation and decide to take action early to increase the chances of the victim's full recovery and survival.

Scanning

Scanning is a combination of eye movement, head movement, body position, and alertness strategies that allow you to watch every area of the water that you are responsible for. This chapter describes zones, emphasizes the importance of your scanning location and ability to see underwater, and explains the use of rotations to keep you alert as you continuously guard the water. This information allows you to develop a scanning method that is effective in your particular work environment. This chapter also explains how to use communication signals to notify others if you see an emergency situation while scanning.

Zones

A *zone* refers to the area of the water you are responsible for when scanning. A zone is three dimensional and includes the water surface, the bottom, and everything in between. No matter where patrons are located or the number of patrons in your zone, the physical area that you scan does not change.

You should be able to describe the exact boundaries of your zone. Your primary zone is the physical area you are responsible for, and your secondary zone is everything within range of your sense of sight, sound, and smell. If you work at a facility with several lifeguards, the water area is divided into multiple zones with overlapping coverage. If you are the only lifeguard at your facility, your zone is the entire pool. The size of the zone you are responsible for may change with the conditions at your facility. You also must be aware of transition zones and how to handle zone coverage during a rotation and during an aquatic emergency.

Zone Size

A zone should be of a size that you can do the following:

- Scan the three-dimensional area within 10 seconds
- Get to the farthest part of the zone within 20 seconds

Zone size at your facility may change based on the number of patrons, the nature of pool activities, the time of day, or other conditions. For example, as more patrons enter your zone, it may take longer to scan or longer to swim across because of the crowded conditions. If the zone can't be scanned in 10 seconds, or if you don't think you could get to the farthest area of the zone within 20 seconds, the zone should be made smaller by adding another lifeguard and reassigning the zones.

Zone charts that clearly mark the location of each protection zone should be posted in the lifeguard office or on the stands. A common method to indicate specific zones is to assign each zone configuration a color code and post zone charts for each. For example, zone assignments when two lifeguards are on duty may be code yellow. Later in the day, when the facility is more crowded and additional lifeguards are on duty, the zone assignments switch to code red. Management decides the code assignments.

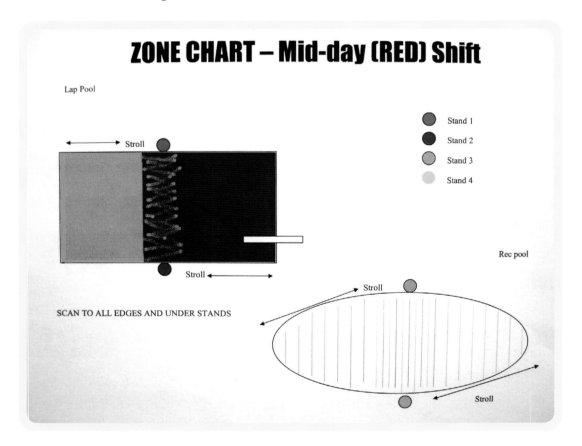

Transition Zones

When more than one activity takes place in a facility, many facilities use a transition zone, or safety zone, such as an area between swimming and diving activities or swimming and boating areas. Participants are not allowed in this zone. Even though this area is not used, it is still part of your zone, and you should scan it just as thoroughly as if swimmers were present.

Emergency Zone Coverage

Be prepared to cover another lifeguard's zone if he or she enters the water to make a rescue. When lifeguards scan adjacent zones, it is usually the lifeguard to the rescuer's left who takes over the zone. Follow the plan in place at your workplace.

When you scan during emergency coverage, watch for a signal for assistance from the lifeguard making the rescue. If he or she needs help, transfer emergency zone coverage to another lifeguard or clear the zone of swimmers according to the plan in place at your facility.

Now that you understand the concept of zones, let's look at scanning methods for effectively monitoring your zone.

Scanning Methods

Constant visual contact with the water, including dedicated attention to the activity in and around it (surveillance), is your primary responsibility. The two key words in this statement are *constant* and *dedicated.*

Over the last two decades, several developments have expanded the scanning process for lifeguards, and they can help you become more effective. Tom Griffiths, the creator of the 5-Minute Scanning Strategy, summarizes these contributions by relating them to the why, when, where, and how of scanning.

- Why. The RID factor reinforces the fact that a drowning victim may be difficult to recognize.
- When. The 10/20 rule, developed by the aquatic safety consulting firm Jeff Ellis and Associates, says that you should be able to scan your entire zone in 10 seconds, and you should be able to reach the farthest point in 20 seconds.
- Where. 3-D triage scanning, developed by the Starfish Aquatics Institute, states that the person who most urgently needs rescue is the one who is submerged and may be on or near the bottom.
- How. The 5-Minute Scanning Strategy provides a systematic method for remaining alert.

Let's look at 3-D triage scanning and the 5-Minute Scanning Strategy more closely.

3-D Triage Scanning

In the medical field, the term *triage* refers to sorting patients in order to be able to provide treatment first to those with the most severe illness or injury. In your zone, where would the most severely endangered victim—one with the most critical need—be located? Remember that once the drowning process has begun and a victim is submerged and cannot breathe, it takes just a few minutes before brain damage or death occurs. Thus, the most critical victims are those who have already completely submerged and drifted toward the bottom.

Triage your scanning by first looking for anything out of the ordinary on the bottom and under the surface (vitally urgent). Then scan looking for other distress or drowning indications from persons on the surface (urgent). Then scan looking for behavior situations that may require rule enforcement (important).

5-Minute Scanning Strategy

This strategy keeps your scanning efforts organized and your attentiveness high. Follow these steps to perform the 5-Minute Scanning Strategy:

1. Consistently scan your zone, sweeping your eyes and turning your head so that you can see every area of the zone every 10 seconds.

2. Use the same scanning pattern for five minutes. A scanning pattern is an organized system that you follow when you sweep your eyes across the zone. Maintaining a scanning pattern helps you stay alert and provide consistent coverage of all areas of your zone. Common scanning patterns include sweeping your eyes side to side or up and down as you look at sections of your zone.

3. As you scan, triage your efforts and first look at the bottom and under the water. Then assess the patrons in your zone that are on the surface and look for behaviors that may indicate distress or drowning.

4. Every five minutes, change posture, position, and pattern. The goal of these changes is to keep you alert through physical movement and mental activity.

Used with permission of Dr. Tom Griffiths.

Make significant position and posture changes by switching from sitting to standing then to strolling. For example, during the first five minutes of your rota-

Side-to-side scanning pattern.

Up-and-down scanning pattern.

Zone sectioning.

tion, sit. During the next five minutes, stand. Then stroll for the next five minutes. Alternate between sitting and standing if strolling is not practical.

If your facility has elevated lifeguard stands with only a small step for your feet, it may not be practical to stand or stroll. In this instance, you will have to identify other ways to meet the objective of keeping alert through physical movement.

A strategy for keeping your mind active and focused is to think about which patrons or places in your zone may be high risk, and visually make contact with these patrons and places during your scan. Next, mentally rehearse a rescue.

Your facility may have a communication system in place so that you can signal to other lifeguards at the end of each five-minute scan that your zone is okay. Common signals used during the five-minute scan to indicate that the zone is OK include a raised "thumbs-up," a raised rescue tube, or a short whistle blast (see Communications Signals on page 53). Other scanning strategies may be necessary in situations where you cannot see the bottom, such as in a waterfront or wilderness setting (see chapter 15).

You can't provide constant and dedicated surveillance for one zone for an extended period; it becomes physically and mentally too difficult. To give you breaks away from surveillance responsibilities, your facility should have a system for frequently moving lifeguards from one location to another. When another lifeguard comes to take over your zone, this change is called a rotation.

Proactive Rotations

Rotations help you keep your attention level high. The shorter your time at a zone and the more frequent your rotations, the more attentive you are likely to be. Rotations generally begin with the lifeguard on break coming back into a lifeguard zone and the other lifeguards moving in sequence to new locations. Rotation timing varies from facility to facility, but it generally occurs every 15 minutes to every hour. Rotation charts (like those shown here) diagram the movement of the lifeguards from station to station.

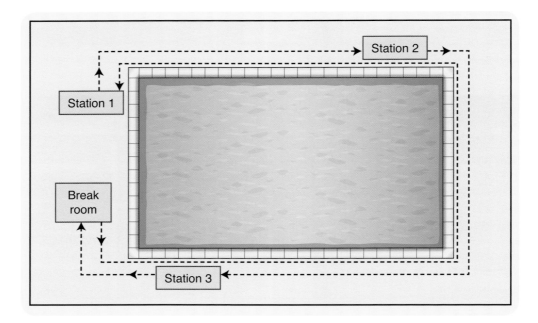

The lifeguard taking over a zone is known as the incoming guard, and the lifeguard who has been scanning the zone is the outgoing guard. A well-performed rotation presents a very professional image and does not compromise the level of surveillance for the zone. A well-executed rotation

- occurs quickly,
- involves limited conversation, and
- provides a systematic transfer of responsibility.

A proactive rotation begins the minute you begin to proceed to your station. Depending upon the features present at your facility, your station may be a lifeguard stand of some type, a slide tower, an in-water location, or a roving position. Scan the water as you walk toward the zone so that you can get a feel for the activity level and begin to prepare yourself mentally for your scanning responsibility. Scanning the zone before you take it over assures that you are becoming responsible for a "clean" zone—one that does not have a drowning victim on the bottom that the previous lifeguard missed.

If you don't have your own rescue tube as you rotate into a station (see chapter 9 for a description of a rescue tube), the outgoing lifeguard will have to transfer one to you. The lifeguard with the rescue tube during a rotation is responsible for scanning and would be the person to make a rescue, if needed.

The procedure description that follows is for a traditional lifeguard stand with several stairs along the back or front. In this procedure the rescue tube is transferred twice. If your facility has lifeguard stands that allow a side, front, or back walkout, you can modify the rotation system so that the tube is transferred once.

The incoming lifeguard performs a full sweep and scan of the bottom of the pool, then says "bottom clear."

The outgoing lifeguard passes the rescue tube to the incoming lifeguard.

The incoming lifeguard positions the rescue tube, begins scanning, and says, "I have the zone."

The outgoing lifeguard climbs down from the chair and stands next to the incoming lifeguard. Both lifeguards scan. The rescue tube is passed back to the outgoing lifeguard, who positions the rescue tube and assumes responsibility by saying, "I have the zone."

The incoming lifeguard climbs up into the chair. The outgoing lifeguard passes the rescue tube back up to the incoming lifeguard, who positions the rescue tube, begins scanning and says, "I have the zone."

The outgoing lifeguard does a complete sweep and scan of the bottom, then says (or signals), "bottom clear" and leaves the zone.

If both of you have a rescue tube, perform the rotation in the same manner except for the transfer of the rescue tube. Be careful to avoid slipping while climbing up or down a chair ladder.

A proactive rotation does not end when you leave the lifeguard stand. Scan the zone as you walk away. Remember that the eyes of the patrons are on you any time you are in public view; maintain your professionalism.

Other factors to consider when planning a scanning strategy are your location, which can affect your ability to see the full three-dimensional volume of water in your zone, and how to communicate to others if you see an emergency situation.

Locations for Lifeguards

The ideal location for scanning is a place where you can see your entire zone. This may be from an elevated lifeguard stand, or an alternate location may be better if the stand has blind spots or a glare problem from the sun during certain times of the day. If you can't see the entire three-dimensional area of your zone from your position, it is your responsibility to move so that you can see or notify your supervisor that you need assistance. In some conditions, the only way you may be able to cover your zone is by roaming the deck and scanning the water while you walk.

Underwater Surveillance

Crowds, glare, ripples, blind spots, or floating rafts and tubes can make it difficult for you to see beneath the surface and scan the area that you know is vitally important. Recent technology makes it possible to scan the underwater area and bottom with a clear view. This new technology greatly increases your ability to spot a swimmer in difficulty and execute a rescue.

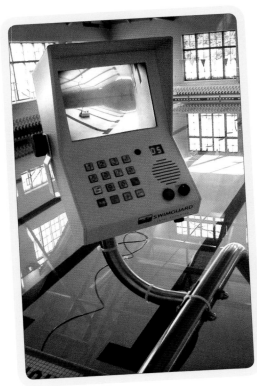

Underwater cameras can be linked to a small monitor on your guard chair, which gives you a view of the bottom to include in your scanning pattern. Do not sit and watch the screen; rather, look at the monitor about every 10 seconds as part of your regular scan. The monitor can be programmed to sound a reminder beep at a designated interval and to track compliance when you push a button to verify that you have looked at the underwater view on the screen.

This technology greatly enhances your ability to see under the water and provide 3-D triage scanning. In some facilities, reliable and user-friendly technology may be the only answer to full and effective water surveillance. This photo shows the underwater view a camera provides.

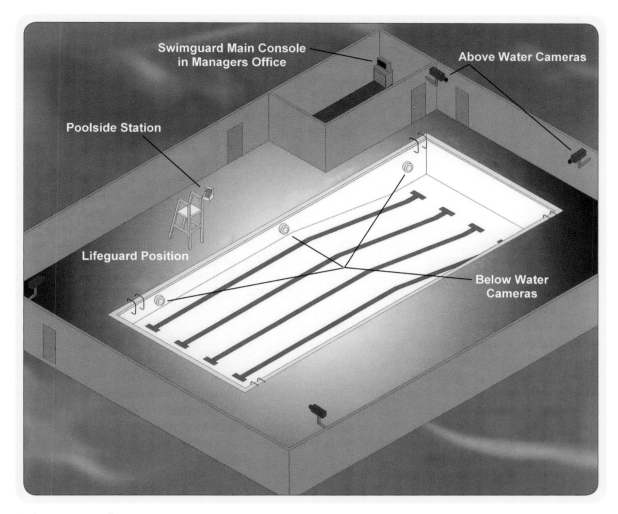

Underwater surveillance system components.

Communication Signals

Clear communication signals are vital to the operation of an aquatic facility. Your facility should have a system of communication signals that allow you to indicate that a rescue is in progress, call for help, request coverage of your zone, and activate the emergency action plan (EAP).

Most communication signals are based on a combination of whistle and hand movements. At a minimum, you should have a whistle with you at all times. Know and practice the communication signals designed for your workplace. Table 6.1 provides a list of communication signals that should be in place and some of the most common signals used.

Table 6.1 Signals for Emergency Communication

Type of emergency	Commonly used signals
Standard rescue	Long whistle blast or air-horn blast
Major rescue (e.g., unconscious person)	2 long whistle blasts or air horn blasts
I need help	Raised fist
I need another lifeguard's attention	2 short whistle blasts
Cover my zone	2 short whistle blasts; tap top of head
Clear the pool or area	Series of long or short whistle blasts
Zone clear and covered, resume activity	Thumbs up

StarGuard Performance Goal

Provide constant and dedicated surveillance using the Starfish scanning model:

- RID factor knowledge
- 10/20 rule
- 5-minute strategy
- 3-D triage
- Proactive rotation

StarGuard Best Practices

- Scan to cover all areas of your zone, including corners, along all walls, and all the way to the bottom.
- Move your eyes and your head when you scan.
- Scan the entire zone, including the bottom, before taking over or leaving a zone during rotation.
- Use the 5-Minute Scanning Strategy to remain alert.
- Scan every area of your zone every 10 seconds.
- Use signals to communicate an emergency.

PART III

Emergency Care

Objectives

Knowledge	Skill	Execution
After reading part III (and the required *Essentials in Emergency Care* text), you should understand the following:	After instructor-observed practice, you should be able to demonstrate the following:	After scenario and site-specific training, you should be able to do the following:
The roles of the various people who respond to emergencies The chain-of-survival concept and components of the Starfish Survival Model The importance of early activation of emergency medical systems (EMS) The development and role of the 9-1-1 system The criteria for determining when to call 9-1-1 and the sequence of events that will happen when you call The limitations when dialing 9-1-1 on a cell phone The legal considerations when providing emergency care The symptoms and common causes of illness or injury in an aquatic environment The conditions that raise suspicion of head, neck, or spinal injuries The symptoms of head, neck, or spinal injuries The objectives of managing a spinal injury on land The standing takedown method of managing a spinal injury The basic treatment for injuries or medical problems The types of pocket masks and their use The methods for performing basic life support for an adult, child, and infant based on the 2005 guidelines for CPR. The methods for opening an obstructed airway for an adult, child, and infant The usefulness of and safety precautions for adjunct equipment, including emergency oxygen, bag-valve masks, automated external defibrillators (AED), manual suction devices	In-line stabilization Standing takedown on land Initial and secondary assessment Sequence for applying a pressure bandage and controlling bleeding Immobilization of an injured limb Open and maintain an airway; check for breathing and circulation Recovery position Adult CPR Child CPR Infant CPR Obstructed-airway management for adult, child, and infant Use of bag-valve masks Use of manual suction devices Use of emergency oxygen Use of an AED	Activate the EMS system as needed Provide basic care for injuries including: *Bleeding* *Sprains, dislocations, and fractures* *Burns* *Suspected head, neck, and spine injury* Provide basic care for medical emergencies and sudden illnesses including: *Heat cramps, heat exhaustion, and heatstroke* *Hypothermia* *Allergic reaction* *Choking* *Seizure* *Heart attack* *Stroke* *Shock* *Diabetic emergency* *Vomiting and fainting* *Bites and stings* *Altered levels of consciousness* *Drowning* Provide basic life support (BLS) for an adult, child, or infant according to the 2005 emergency cardiac care guidelines, with or without adjunct equipment

Contacting Emergency Medical Systems

A medical emergency, such as a sudden illness or injury, can happen at any time. A coordinated response by the people and agencies that provide care offers the best chance for a good outcome. This chapter provides information about the Starfish Survival Model based on the concept of chain of survival, describes the roles of those who might respond to an emergency, and describes how and when to contact emergency medical systems (EMS).

The goal of emergency care is to provide the best possible chance for an ill or injured person to survive with the fewest long-term effects. When an emergency happens, responders may provide different levels of care, depending on the severity of the event and their training.

Responder Chain of Command

The training level of those who respond to an emergency can vary widely. When trained personnel are not present, Good Samaritans are bystanders who choose to provide care. These individuals usually have had some type of training in CPR or first aid through courses taught in school or at another community location. People trained in basic life support (BLS) and basic first aid at the first-responder level (such as lifeguards) can provide care in the critical time after an emergency occurs and before EMS arrives. First responders might also be trained to use equipment such as emergency oxygen and automated external defibrillators (AED). Those who are trained at this level often have jobs in which they have a "duty to act" if

an emergency occurs, and they are often first on the scene and are responsible for calling EMS.

An emergency medical system consists of people with various types of training who respond when 9-1-1 is called. EMS units are usually staffed with emergency medical technicians (EMTs) or paramedics. Emergency medical technicians have completed extensive hours of advanced training, particularly in advanced cardiac life support (ACLS), and they can perform additional emergency medical procedures under the authorization of a physician designated as a medical director for the local EMS unit. Paramedics are additionally trained to use specialized equipment, administer medications, and perform medical procedures under the direction of a physician.

The care that any of these people provide is prehospital care because it takes place either at the site of the emergency or in an ambulance on the way to the hospital. The EMS responders decide whether or not to transport an ill or injured person to a hospital for additional care. Once at the hospital, if necessary, the emergency room medical team can provide advanced life support care. This medical team may determine that additional specialized care is necessary and transfer the injured or ill person to another hospital, such as a regional trauma center.

When an emergency occurs at an aquatic facility, particularly if it involves an unconscious drowning victim, a coordinated response is important. You, as a lifeguard, are the first link in this chain of survival, and the victim's survival depends on how quickly he or she progresses through the sequence of events. Years of research have determined the steps in the chain-of-survival concept. These actions make a difference in the survival of an injured or ill person, especially one in cardiac arrest. These actions include the following:

- Early activation of EMS
- Early CPR
- Early defibrillation
- Early advanced life support

For response to an aquatic emergency, the Starfish Survival Model adds the lifeguard response and early recognition to the chain.

Slow response in any area lessens the chance of a good outcome. Because EMS response plays such a large role in emergency care, let's look at the information you must know before calling EMS and some details about the EMS system, provided by the National Academies of Emergency Dispatch.

Early Recognition
Scan
Target
Assess
Alert
Rescue

Early advanced life support

Early activation

Improved survival

Early defibrillation

Early CPR

Starfish survival model.

Early Activation of Emergency Medical Systems

Early activation of EMS is a critical component in the chain of survival. Knowing how to call EMS from the facility where you work is an important component of your lifeguard responsibilities. Most communities use 9-1-1 as the emergency number for calling EMS, although a few still use special seven-digit emergency numbers. For successful early activation, the following should occur:

- All staff members must know how to dial out if your facility requires special access to an outside line. For example, in many situations you must first dial 9 to get a line before dialing 9-1-1.

- The name, address, and phone number of your facility should be posted next to all telephones.

- If the emergency number is something besides 9-1-1, all staff members must memorize the number and the dialing instructions, and the emergency number should be posted next to all phones.

Many 9-1-1 agencies have enhanced computerized systems that instantly provide the dispatcher with the address and telephone number of the caller if the person is calling from a landline phone. However, this system does not work with wireless or cell phones. A federal government project is under way to make sure that calls for help made from cell phones in the United States will be routed to the closest public safety agency for proper dispatch and that the location of the calls can be more accurately determined. Although in the future 9-1-1 agencies may be able to locate you if you call from a cell phone, for now it is your responsibility when calling on a cell phone to identify your location by a street name, a street number, a landmark, or directions. If you do not know your location, the dispatcher will work with you to help determine your exact location or where to send help.

Background on 9-1-1

The 9-1-1 emergency number got its start in the 1970s as a way for people to get assistance more easily. Before the use of 9-1-1, people had to use a seven-digit number to call for help. Time spent looking up emergency numbers, panicked misdialing, and failure to verify the true location of the emergency often caused unnecessary delays in getting help. Today, as a testament to success of the 9-1-1 program, nearly 93 percent of all municipalities in the United States have implemented this service.

Source: National Emergency Number Association (NENA)

When to Call 9-1-1 for Help

Research has shown that people have difficulty recognizing medical emergencies or underestimate the seriousness of emergencies and fail to call for help. Remember, if you *think* you or someone you know is experiencing a medical emergency, call 9-1-1 immediately. If someone experiences any of the following, you should call 9-1-1:

- A snakebite
- A bee sting that causes a reaction
- An allergic reaction of any kind
- A seizure or convulsion
- Uncontrollable jerking movements
- Burns over an area larger than the palm of your hand
- Electrical burn or shock
- Severe injury, trauma, or an attack
- Bleeding or spurting blood that you can't stop
- Difficulty breathing or cessation of breathing
- Gasping for air or turning blue or purple
- Choking and the inability to clear the obstruction
- Unconsciousness, fainting, lack of alertness, and emission of strange noises
- Chest pains, chest pressure or constriction, or crushing discomfort around the chest (even if the pain stops)
- Unusual numbness, tightness, pressure, or aching pain in the chest, neck, jaw, arm, or upper back

The signs and symptoms of a medical emergency can be vague or unusual. For example, the classic symptom associated with heart attack is an uncomfortable, dull feeling of pressure or tightness in the chest. However, some people experiencing a heart attack may simply feel light-headed, short of breath, or sick to the stomach, or they might break out in a cold sweat. These less well-known heart attack symptoms might be dismissed as a minor illness.

Another reason that people fail to call 9-1-1 in an emergency is that ill or injured people frequently refuse to accept that something is wrong. They may feel that the illness is not serious enough for a call to 9-1-1, or they may be worried about the long-term effect the emergency might have on such things as work, child care, or finances. They want to believe that they are OK, so they try to convince themselves that they don't need emergency help. Providing help in an emergency may involve acting in the face of uncertainty. You may have to force yourself to take action even though you are not sure that a real emergency exists or when the sick or injured person actively denies that he or she needs help. **Never be afraid to dial 9-1-1 just because you are unsure a real emergency exists.** Dial 9-1-1 and let the dispatch center and emergency service professionals help you in times of confusion or doubt. That's what they are there for.

What to Expect When You Call 9-1-1

Typically, a professional emergency dispatcher with specialized training to deal with crises over the phone will answer your 9-1-1 call. Be prepared to briefly and accurately explain your situation. Many dispatchers today are trained to provide real-time instruction in CPR and lifesaving first aid while simultaneously dispatching emergency medical service professionals to your location. Listen to the dispatcher and follow his or her instructions.

Most public safety agencies have access to a variety of highly trained personnel and specialized equipment and vehicles. To ensure that the right people with the right equipment are sent to the correct location, the 9-1-1 dispatcher must ask you specific questions. Sometimes it may seem that the dispatcher is asking these questions to determine whether or not you need help. In actuality, he or she is asking them to determine the level of help you need. Remember, trained dispatchers never ask unnecessary questions.

The dispatcher will always ask you to state the address of the emergency and your callback number for verification. You must state this information (or state it twice if there is no computerized 9-1-1 screen) to be sure that the dispatcher hears it and copies it down correctly. The dispatcher knows how important it is to do it right and not just fast. The dispatcher asks four universal questions in order to put his or her knowledge and experience to work for you quickly and effectively after he or she has verified the address and callback telephone number at the emergency site:

1. Exactly what happened (person's problem or type of incident)?
2. What is the victim's approximate age?
3. Is he or she conscious?
4. Is he or she breathing?

Getting this critical information from you typically takes less than 30 seconds. After that, you may be asked to do nothing, to get out of an unsafe environment, or to stay on the line and assist in providing care for the ill or injured person. Working with 9-1-1 callers, emergency medical dispatchers (EMDs), professionals trained to provide telephone instruction in CPR and lifesaving first aid, have helped save thousands of lives during the first 5 to 10 minutes it usually takes EMS professionals to arrive at the scene of an emergency.

In all cases, remember that the most important thing you can do when calling 9-1-1 is to *listen carefully.* Always do whatever the dispatcher asks you to do. Don't tell him or her to hurry; he or she already knows that. Every question the dispatcher asks is asked for an important reason; that's why it's in the protocol.

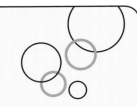

StarGuard Performance Goal

When an emergency occurs, follow the Starfish Survival Model:

- Early recognition
- Early activation of EMS
- Early CPR
- Early defibrillation
- Early advanced life support

StarGuard Best Practices

- Know what to dial to reach EMS from your facility.
- Know the address of your facility, especially if you call from a cell phone.
- State exactly what happened and listen carefully.

Providing Emergency Care

Your first aid training has prepared you to provide basic care for a variety of illnesses and injuries, and you know when and how to call EMS. This chapter helps you understand some of the legal considerations related to providing emergency care, and it summarizes the most common illnesses and injuries that happen in an aquatic environment so that you know what to expect when you lifeguard. This chapter also discusses the causes and symptoms of head, neck, and spinal injuries and shows you how to manage this type of injury until EMS arrives. Because a person with a suspected spinal injury at an aquatic facility is often found in a standing position, this chapter describes how to perform a technique called the standing takedown.

Legal Considerations

During an emergency, certain medical and legal principles apply to what you are expected to do. These principles include the following:

- Duty to act. You have an obligation to provide emergency care.
- Consent. You must obtain the permission of the person before giving emergency care.

Note: This chapter is supplemented with the American Safety and Health Institute first aid curriculum materials.

- Expressed consent. People over the age of 18 may give oral or written consent or give consent by gesturing.

- Implied consent. If someone is unable to request help and requires medical attention, as in the case of someone who is unconscious, it is assumed that he or she would give consent for you to provide emergency care.

- Standard of care. This is the level of emergency care that you are expected to provide, based on the level of your emergency care training (e.g., basic life support, advanced life support).

- Confidentiality. A person has the right for his or her name and medical history to remain confidential among care providers. Care providers may share only information pertinent to medical care. The regulation that governs confidentiality is the Health Insurance Portability and Accountability Act, which is commonly referred to as the HIPAA law.

- Negligence. This occurs when an injured or ill person incurs proven damage from a trained person who has a duty to act and the person does not uphold the standard of care.

- Good Samaritan laws. These laws, which vary from state to state, protect people from litigation (lawsuits) if they were a bystander and did not have a duty to act, but chose to help. In order to be protected under these laws, a bystander must give reasonable aid.

- Refusal of care. A person older than 18 can refuse treatment and care if he or she is alert and oriented to the surroundings.

- Documentation. All emergency care provided must be recorded in writing. This document serves as a medical record and legal documentation.

More details about legal liability are explained in chapter 13. Let's now look at some of the situations for which you may need to provide care when you are lifeguarding.

Common Illnesses and Injuries

The more patrons that come through your gates every day, the more likely it is that some will have preexisting medical conditions that could cause them to become ill at your facility. And even with prevention strategies in place, injuries occur. Table 8.1 provides a summary of the most frequent types of incidents that happen at an aquatic facility, along with their causes.

An injured person may come to you in a standing position on land; it is common for a person to hit his or her head, stand up, and not realize right away that he or she is injured. Therefore, you must know the conditions and symptoms that might indicate a spinal injury.

Managing Spinal Injuries on Land

A spinal injury can create permanent paralysis and change a person's life in a matter of seconds. Because you have no way to diagnose the extent of an injury, the objective any time you suspect a spinal injury is to minimize the movement of the head, neck, and spine while maintaining the person's ability to breathe. You will do this until EMS arrives.

Table 8.1   Common Injuries and Illnesses in an Aquatic Environment

Illness or injury	Common causes
Split chin, lip, or forehead	Collision with pool edge, deck, or another patron
Scraped knee; sprained or broken limb	Slipping and falling, usually caused by running
Nosebleed	Getting bumped by another patron
Knocked-out or chipped tooth	Collision with pool edge or another patron
Temperature-related illness (hypothermia, hyperthermia)	Staying in the water or sun too long; dehydration
Head, neck, or spinal injury	Collision with pool bottom, side, diving board, or another patron; fall from a height
Allergic reaction	Insect or wildlife bite or sting
Vomiting	Swallowing too much water, overexertion, heat exhaustion, or illness
Life-threatening medical emergency (e.g., heart attack, stroke, seizure, asthma attack, diabetic emergency)	Known or unknown preexisting medical condition

Special precautions are required if you suspect a spinal injury. Activities that might cause a spinal injury include the following:

- Falling from a height greater than the person's height
- Forcefully striking the head on the bottom of the pool
- Suffering a severe blow to the head, neck, or back as a result of collision with another person, equipment, or hard surface

Based on documented rescue statistics, people who have suffered a head, neck, or spinal injury at a facility with prevention strategies and lifeguards in place are usually conscious. A person who is unconscious should not be considered to have a spinal injury unless there was some action that causes you to suspect that a spinal injury occurred. This action is known as a "mechanism of injury." For example, a lap swimmer found unconscious in the middle of the pool should not be suspected of having a spinal injury, because there was no reasonable way that a traumatic injury would have occurred. Certain symptoms suggest a head, neck, or spinal injury. These symptoms can show up immediately or they could be delayed. Suspect a head, neck, or spinal injury if a patron exhibits any of the following:

- Altered consciousness, confusion, slowed thinking
- Difficulty breathing
- Impaired vision
- Inability to move a body part
- Headache
- Vomiting
- Loss of balance

- Pain
- Tingling or numbness in hands, fingers, feet, or toes

Unless there are life-threatening conditions, *never* move an injured person who is on land or allow them to attempt to move. However, you can use the standing takedown technique to lower someone with a suspected spinal injury to the ground. This procedure brings the person to the ground, which helps avoid additional injury from a fall, should the person become unable to stand.

Standing Takedown

You must take immediate action if someone walks up to you complaining of pain and symptoms that indicate a spinal injury. If EMS response time is short, you might not need to perform a standing takedown and may simply minimize

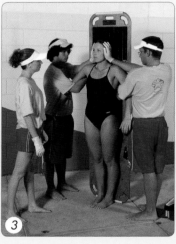

Identify yourself to the person and ask him or her for permission to provide care. Put on gloves and signal for help and for a backboard before making contact with the injured person because once you begin to stabilize the person's head, you cannot let go. Talk to the injured person throughout the process and tell him or her what to expect from each step before you perform it. Tell the person to respond to your questions with verbal answers, rather than nodding or shaking their head.

Place your open hands on either side of the person's head and extend your arms down his or her chest. Position yourself slightly off center in case the person vomits. The backup rescuers place the backboard behind the person.

The backup rescuers secure the person to the backboard by reaching under his or her armpit and grasping the backboard handhold. The backup rescuers take control of the person's head by placing the fingers of their free hands between yours. As both rescuers begin to apply even pressure, you begin to slide your hands down and out.

Move to the back of the backboard and grasp the top of the board at the handhold. Make sure there is enough room behind you to lower the backboard. If not, consider having everyone rotate as a unit, maintaining stabilization of the person's head and taking small steps either to the left or right. Turn about three inches at a time until there is room to lower the board.

movement until EMS arrives. However, a person with a spinal injury may begin to have swelling of the brain stem, which could cause the person's legs to be unable to support his or her body. Lower the person to a horizontal position on the ground to keep the person from collapsing and to prevent possible additional injury. Use the procedures shown here to perform a standing takedown.

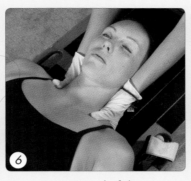

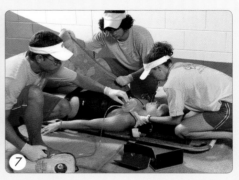

On your count (say "Ready, on three. One, two, three."), all of you lower the backboard slowly into a horizontal position. You control the descent of the board while the other rescuers walk down into a kneeling position as the board lowers, maintaining even pressure against the person's head.

Now regain control of the person's head by sliding your fingers and palms under the person's shoulders and placing your thumbs over the shoulders. The other rescuers should maintain stabilization of the head. Slide your forearms along the person's head, applying even pressure, as the backup rescuers remove their hands.

Until EMS arrives, maintain this position while monitoring the person's condition. Keep the person warm and apply emergency oxygen, if available.

You can also use the standing takedown to extricate a person who is standing in shallow water, such as in a catch pool at the bottom of a waterslide. See chapter 10 for procedures to manage a person with a suspected spinal injury when he or she is in the water.

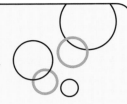

StarGuard Performance Goal

Provide basic care for minor injuries or illnesses and provide emergency care from the time the incident occurs until EMS arrives.

StarGuard Best Practices

- Identify yourself and ask permission to provide care to an ill or injured person.
- Talk to an injured or ill person to keep him or her aware of what you are doing.
- Suspect a spinal injury if the person was engaged in an activity that could cause a spinal injury or if the person has symptoms of a spinal injury.
- If spinal injury is suspected, minimize movement of the head, neck, and spine while maintaining the person's ability to breathe until EMS arrives.
- When indicated, use the standing takedown to lower a standing person with a suspected spinal injury into a horizontal position.

Aquatic Rescue

Objectives

Knowledge	Skill	Execution
After reading part IV, you should understand the following:	After instructor-observed practice, you should be able to demonstrate the following:	After scenario and site-specific training, you should be able to do the following:
The method for using basic rescue equipment for land-based rescues and assists The advantages of using a rescue tube for an in-water rescue The importance of minimizing body-to-body contact and maintaining a safe position during a rescue The minimum equipment that should be present at every aquatic facility The STAAR Aquatic Rescue Model The methods for activating the emergency action plan for a water rescue The water entry from the deck or a height The water entry for rescuing someone with a suspected spinal injury The characteristics of an effective approach stroke The considerations when making contact with a distressed or drowning person The principles of escape from a panicked person How to complete a report after a rescue The objectives of rescuing multiple victims or injured people The considerations when using the leg-wrap rescue in deep water The objectives of rescuing a person having a seizure The techniques for providing in-water, in-line stabilization for a person with a suspected spinal injury	Land-based assist Compact jump Approach stroke Feetfirst surface dive Emergency escape Use of a rescue tube for: *Front rescue* *Rear rescue* *Two-guard rescue* *Leg-wrap (and extended) rescues* *Multiple-victim and injured person rescues* In-water spinal-injury techniques for in-line stabilization: *Ease-in entry* *Vise grip* *Vise-grip rollover* *Change-up* *Alternative vise-grip rollover* *Ease-up to vise-grip* *Spinal rollover*	Provide aquatic rescue for a conscious distressed swimmer or drowning victim Provide aquatic rescue and basic life support for an unconscious drowning victim based on the 2005 CPR guidelines Provide in-water management of a suspected spinal injury according to site-specific guidelines based on local EMS protocol Supplement care with adjunct equipment (oxygen, BVM, suction, AED), if available

(continued)

(continued)

Knowledge	Skill	Execution
The objectives of backboarding and extrication The site-specific considerations of backboarding The method for rescue breathing in the water The technique for using a backboard to extricate an unconscious person from the water The considerations for integrating adjunct equipment into a rescue in progress The basic life support (BLS) considerations for drowning victims The rescue protocols for unconscious drowning victims based on the 2005 CPR guidelines The precautions for minimizing movement and the priority of care if spinal injury is suspected if a person is unconscious	Backboarding and extrication techniques: *Change-up* *Two-guard backboarding* *Team backboarding* *Standing takedown in shallow water* Techniques for rescuing an unconscious victim: *Rescue breathing in the water* *Backboard pullout or walkout* *On-land emergency care and basic life support*	

Assists and Rescues

If you are able to recognize distress or drowning symptoms soon after they begin, it is likely that the majority of the people you rescue will be conscious. In this chapter we discuss how to rescue someone who is conscious. We start by examining the various types of rescue equipment, a model for performing rescues, and the basics of activating an emergency action plan. We then talk about how to perform land-based rescues or assists, followed by the details of how to enter the water and approach a distressed person or drowning victim, execute a rescue, remove the person from the water, and report the incident.

Rescue Equipment

Most state health department regulations require aquatic facilities to have basic rescue equipment, such as a reaching pole, ring buoy, and telephone, readily available for emergency use by untrained bystanders. Lifeguards generally use a rescue tube to perform rescues. A rescue tube is a length of dense foam fitted with a strap. A rescue tube is usually 42 to 54 inches long (107 to 137 centimeters), 6 inches tall (15 centimeters), and 4 inches thick (10 centimeters). Rescue tubes are designed for use by trained aquatic rescuers, and you should have one with you whenever you are on duty. The rescue tube will do the following:

- Provide flotation support for you
- Provide flotation support for the distressed swimmer or drowning victim

- Eliminate body-to-body contact with the distressed swimmer or drowning victim
- Improve the likelihood of a successful rescue

Rescue tubes have revolutionized the ability of lifeguards to make safe and effective rescues in a wide range of conditions. Rescue tubes provide an excellent means of flotation and can support several people at one time. Rescue tubes level the playing field by making it possible for a small lifeguard to effectively manage a large drowning victim or for a lifeguard to manage more than one person at a time. In addition to rescue tubes, and other equipment that your local health department requires, your aquatic facility should have the following equipment on hand:

- Backboard or extrication device
- First aid kit
- Personal protection equipment such as gloves and barrier mask
- Biohazard cleanup kit
- Telephone

A variety of additional, or adjunct, emergency response equipment is available. Your facility's protocols, emergency action plan, and your level of training determine your use of adjunct equipment. This equipment might include the following:

- Emergency oxygen
- Automated external defibrillator (AED)
- Hand-powered suction devices
- Bag-valve mask (BVM)

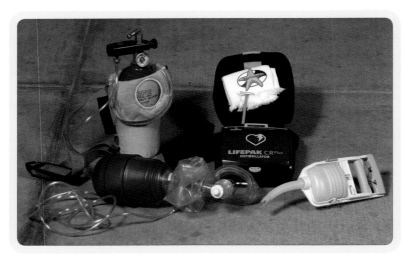

You're now ready to put everything you've learned so far into a system for making an effective rescue. You know how to scan, target, and assess to recognize a distressed swimmer or drowning victim. You have some type of communication device to alert others that you are making a rescue and to activate your facility's emergency action plan. You know how to use the equipment that is available. The next step is to enter the water and make a rescue.

Starfish Aquatic Rescue Model

When an emergency occurs, it is helpful to have a systematic method for responding. Aquatic professionals Kim W. Tyson and Robert E. Ogoreuc developed the STARR (scan, target, assess, remove, report) aquatic rescue model as a way to teach lifeguards how to respond to aquatic emergencies. The Starfish Aquatics Institute has modified the acronym to STAAR (scan, target, assess, alert, rescue) to summarize the key elements you will perform in an aquatic rescue and to include the step of *alert* to activate your emergency action plan and call EMS.

Regardless of whether the person to be rescued is on the surface of the water or submerged, is conscious or unconscious, or is facing toward you or away from you, the steps, which follow, are the same:

Scan the zone.

Target the area with your eyes if you recognize distress or drowning behavior or if something unknown catches your attention.

Assess the situation and decide whether or not to take action.

Alert others with a whistle or other device.

Rescue the person; decide what action to take.

Adapted from Tyson, K. and Ogoreuc, R. S.T.A.R.R.: "Method for Responding to Aquatic Emergencies," *American Lifeguard Magazine.* Winter 2002. P. 15, 17, 18.

When the rescue has been accomplished, the two final steps are to *remove* the person from the water and to complete a rescue *report*. Once the person is out of the water, your role is to monitor his or her condition. If necessary, provide first aid, or if the victim becomes unconscious, basic life support care until EMS arrives. Fill out the rescue report after all necessary emergency care has been provided and before the injured person leaves your facility. If the person is being transported by EMS, obtain as much information as possible and complete the report later.

Chapter 2 explains that an emergency action plan (EAP) is a blueprint for *who* does *what, when* during an emergency. Now let's explore an EAP for an aquatic rescue.

Activating the Emergency Action Plan for a Water Rescue

When you activate the emergency action plan for an aquatic rescue, you put into motion a system of backup and support. Your whistle signal, or other site-specific communication device, alerts others that a rescue is taking place. In multi-guard facilities a rescue team will respond. The members of a rescue team vary from facility to facility, but generally, the lifeguards on break and supervisors on site respond to the EAP signal. Your rescue team's ability to make a successful rescue is only as strong as your weakest rescue team member and is directly related to your team's ability to work together. Therefore, you and your rescue team must simulate real-life situations when practicing the emergency action plan. Rescue team members should be prepared to provide the following assistance:

- Cover your zone while you make the rescue or clear the zone
- Enter the water and assist with the rescue if you signal for help
- Bring equipment to the pool edge, beach entry, or other designated point
- Call 9-1-1 if necessary
- Provide crowd management
- Help remove the person from the water
- Assist with follow-up care or basic life support on deck or on the shore

If you are the only lifeguard available to manage an emergency, your EAP task becomes more difficult. You must be prepared to solicit help from bystanders. Bystanders become your rescue team members, and you must tell them specifically and clearly what to do.

When you have identified a distressed swimmer or drowning victim, you must first determine whether you can help from land. If not, then you must enter the water and perform a water rescue.

Land-Based Assists

If a distressed swimmer is conscious and within reaching distance, it may be faster and just as effective to extend your rescue tube to the person and help from land than to help from the water. The swimmer must be able to see or feel the rescue tube as you extend it toward him or her and must be able to follow your directions to grab the tube. He or she must also have the strength to hold onto the rescue tube until you pull the person to safety.

When you extend a rescue tube to a person in the water, keep your weight shifted back to avoid being pulled in. Be careful not to injure the person with the device as you place it within his or her reach, especially if the rescue tube has a metal clip on the end.

Water Entry and Approach

Entering the water to make a rescue is often the most effective way to manage a conscious distressed swimmer or drowning victim. However, before you make a water rescue, follow the steps of the STAAR Aquatic Rescue Model: scan, target, assess, alert, *and then* rescue.

Always use a rescue tube when making a rescue. Wear the strap diagonally around your chest and keep the tube between you and the person in the water at all times when making a water rescue. To begin a rescue, enter the water using either a compact jump or an ease-in entry, and then swim toward the person with an approach stroke.

Compact-Jump Entry

A compact-jump entry is useful in a wide range of water depths and circumstances. Because you enter the water in a compact position, your risk of back, leg, or foot injury is lower than with other techniques.

A compact jump is best performed into water that is at least as deep as the distance from your takeoff point to the surface of the water where you will enter. Depending on the water depth and the height of your lifeguard stand, it might be best to climb down from the lifeguard stand and enter from the deck. To perform a compact jump, do the following:

Hold the rescue tube tightly across the front of your body with the strap gathered in your hand or tucked behind the tube.

Jump forward and pull your knees up. Lift your toes up so that your body is in a compact position, almost like a "cannonball."

Keep yourself in the compact position until you enter the water. You may submerge momentarily, but the rescue tube will bring you to the surface quickly.

Ease-In Entry

If you suspect that a person has a spinal injury and he or she is close enough to your entry point that the splash of a compact jump would move the person, use an ease-in entry, which won't create a splash. To perform an ease-in entry, follow these steps:

1. Sit on the pool edge.
2. Slip into the water feetfirst.
3. Control the speed and depth of your entry by holding onto the side.

Approach Stroke

Once you are in the water, the objective is to use any combination of arm strokes and leg kicks to make rapid progress toward the person. For example, it may be faster for you to swim using a freestyle arm stroke and kick, or you might prefer a breaststroke, or a combination of the two strokes. Swim with your head up to maintain visual contact while you approach.

Freestyle kick with freestyle pull.

Freestyle kick with breaststroke pull.

Keep the rescue tube under your arms and across your chest if the person is just a few yards or meters away. If you anticipate swimming more than a few yards, it might be faster to trail the tube behind you. When you are about 10 feet (3 meters) from the person, pull the rescue tube into position across your chest.

As you swim toward the person you are rescuing, assess the situation to determine which type of water rescue will be best. Depending on the location of and condition of the person, you may decide to use a front, rear, two-guard, or leg-wrap rescue technique. If more than one person needs assistance, you will manage a multiperson rescue.

Water Rescue

The first objective of a water rescue is to minimize body-to-body contact between you and the person being rescued. Other objectives include the following:

- To keep your head and the head of the person you are rescuing above water so that you both can breathe
- To make progress toward a takeout point, such as a wall, ladder, or zero-depth beach entry area
- To provide safety instructions to a conscious patron to reduce the risk of the incident happening again

A conscious person in distress or drowning will either be facing you or facing away from you. And he or she will be either on the surface or submerged. Use the front rescue if the person is facing you and the rear rescue if the person is facing away from you or if you feel more comfortable making a rescue from behind. Use the two-guard rescue if you need help with a large or very active person and the leg wrap if the person is submerged.

Front Rescue

When making a front rescue you can see the other person's face, which provides you the ability to communicate with them. Also, when you push the rescue tube into the other person's chest, it drives the person backward, minimizing the risk of him or her grabbing you. To perform a front rescue, do the following:

Swim to a position about arm's length in front of the struggling person.

Push the rescue tube *firmly* and *quickly* into the person's chest by quickly extending your arms and locking your elbows. Encourage the person to grab the tube. Keep your arms straight and extended so that the other person is at least an arm's length away from you and on the other side of the rescue tube.

(continued)

(continued)

Keep kicking to continue your forward motion. When the person is calm and maintaining contact with the rescue tube, change direction (if needed) toward the closest wall or exit point.

Studies of actual rescues involving conscious people in distress or drowning victims show that once a person is holding onto the rescue tube and realizes that it provides flotation, he or she stops struggling and panic subsides. However, if a person refuses to grab the rescue tube, back away and try the rescue again. If the person still will not grab the rescue tube, swim to a position behind him or her and use the rear-rescue technique or signal for help from another rescuer and perform a two-guard rescue.

Rear Rescue

To perform a rear rescue, you hold the person securely on the rescue tube. Approaching from behind minimizes the chance of the person grabbing you. To perform a rear rescue, do the following:

Keep the rescue tube at your chest and move directly behind the person. Turn your head to the side so that the struggling person's head movements don't hit your face.

Reach under the person's arms and around his or her chest, then pull the person slightly back onto the tube. Hold the person securely on the tube.

3 Kick to make progress toward the takeout point. If the person is calm and secure on the rescue tube, consider maintaining your grasp around the tube and person with one arm and using your other arm to pull.

Two-Guard Rescue

The two-guard rescue allows you to effectively and safely manage a large or uncontrollable person. This technique combines the front and rear rescues and requires two rescuers. To perform a two-guard rescue, do the following:

If you are the initial rescuer and need assistance, back away from the person and signal for help by raising a clenched fist.

When the other lifeguard arrives, one of you moves behind the struggling person, and the other moves in front. If you are behind, perform a rear rescue and make a "target" with your open hands. If you are in front, perform a front rescue, aiming for the "target." Communicate with your corescuer so that you both perform the front rescue and rear rescue techniques at the same time.

If you are performing the rear rescue, reach over the tube in front of the victim, and pull in tight. If you are performing the front rescue, push forward with extended arms.

Leg-Wrap Rescue

Use the leg-wrap rescue to reach someone underwater. The benefits of this technique include the following:

- There is no upper-body-to-upper-body contact between you and a drowning victim.
- If the drowning victim is struggling and grabs your legs, you can easily escape by pushing the person away using the strength of your legs and feet.

- Because you reach the person with your legs rather than your hands and arms, you don't have to submerge your body as far to make the rescue.
- Your hands are left free, which allows you to maintain contact with the rescue tube. This gives you the ability to use the flotation capability of the tube to bring both you and the other person to the surface without having to swim up.

To perform a leg-wrap rescue, do the following:

Position yourself behind the drowning victim. Hold onto the rescue tube, take a breath of air, and submerge. Maintain your grasp on the rescue tube and extend your arms above your head to lower your body feetfirst, toward the person.

Use your feet and lower legs to grab the person tightly under his or her arms. Rotate your feet to provide contact with the person's upper chest. If the drowning victim is struggling, apply pressure with your lower legs for more control.

Bend your knees and pull the rescue tube toward your chest. These movements will bring you and the other person up to a position on the surface.

4 Reach over the rescue tube and perform a rear rescue.

Some drowning victims may be in deep water and are submerged farther than your legs will reach while holding onto the rescue tube body. In this situation you can use the extended leg-wrap rescue or the superextended leg-wrap rescue.

Extended Leg-Wrap Rescue

If the drowning victim is too deep to be reached with a standard leg wrap, extend your reach by holding onto the tube strap, rather than the tube, when you perform the rescue. The first step in performing the extended leg-wrap rescue is to perform a feetfirst surface dive as follows:

Let go of the body of the rescue tube and make a circle with your thumb and forefinger around the rescue tube strap. Don't grasp the strap; you want it to slide freely. Maintain a vertical body position with your legs together with your toes pointed. Keep your body as tight and streamlined as possible.

Turn your palms so that they face upward and lift your arms up over your head. Push the water up toward the surface so that your body is propelled downward. Maintain loose contact with the rescue tube strap as you lift your arms.

If you need to descend deeper, reposition your hands at your sides to take another pull. To reposition, bend your elbows and pass your hands and arms in front of your body. Lowering your arms this way will help keep your body streamlined and won't break your momentum.

After you have performed a feetfirst surface dive, position yourself above and behind the victim while maintaining contact with the rescue tube strap. Grasp the victim under the arms and around the upper torso with your feet and lower legs. Extend your arm as far up the tube strap as you can reach and grasp the strap. Pull on the tube strap (hand over hand if needed) to bring yourself and the victim toward the surface. As you reach the surface, place the tube across your chest. Bend your knees to bring the victim up to the surface and into a position for a rear rescue.

Superextended Leg-Wrap Rescue

If further extension is needed, remove the body strap from across your chest. Firmly grasp the end of the wide loop. Holding onto the strap, surface dive (feetfirst or headfirst) to a position just above and behind the victim. If you have performed a headfirst surface dive, be sure to reverse yourself before you get within a few feet of the victim so that your legs are positioned downward. Grasp the victim under the armpits and upper torso with your legs and feet. Pull up on the tube strap, hand over hand, to bring yourself and the victim toward the surface. When you reach the surface, position the tube across your chest, then pull the victim up into a rear-rescue position.

Special-Situation Rescues

Sometimes more than one person may need to be rescued at a time or the person being rescued may be injured. In these cases, you need to adapt to the circumstances. By understanding the objectives you need to accomplish—from both a water rescue and first aid standpoint—you can modify the skills you already know to make a successful rescue.

Rescuing Multiple Victims

If more than one person is in distress or drowning at the same time, you must determine if it is safe to attempt a multiperson rescue. Remember that your primary objective is to maintain your safety by not making body-to-body contact. Your secondary objective is to provide the people you are rescuing with flotation so that everyone, including you, remains on the surface and breathes. A rescue tube can provide flotation for several people at once.

There is no step-by-step method for performing a multiperson rescue because each situation is different. Your goal is to get everyone on the rescue tube as quickly as possible

Rescuing an Injured Person

Except in the case of a suspected spinal injury, there is no step-by-step method for rescuing an injured person because each situation is different. Your main objective is to place the injured person on the rescue tube so that he or she remains on the surface and breathes, then you can progress to a takeout point so that you can provide first aid. Minimize movement of an injured area, such as a broken or dislocated arm, as you perform the rescue. When appropriate, begin basic first aid while the person is on the rescue tube on the way to the takeout point. For example, you can apply direct pressure to control bleeding or stabilize a broken arm by holding it against the person's body.

Once you have effectively managed an aquatic rescue and are at the pool wall or shoreline, the next steps are to help the person exit the water, provide follow-up instructions, and complete the paperwork necessary to document the rescue.

Remove and Report

When you get to the takeout point, help the person you rescued exit the water. Take care not to embarrass or call unnecessary attention to the person, but make sure the person understands what caused the situation, and provide safety instructions to reduce the likelihood of the situation happening again.

Methods for removing an injured person from the water in a pool environment are explained in chapter 10 and for an unconscious person in chapter 11. Removal methods useful in a beachfront or wilderness setting are explained in chapter 15.

Document water rescues in a rescue report using clear, concise language. Include follow-up instructions, and obtain all of the requested information so that the report is complete. Avoid stating your opinions of what occurred; stick to the facts. A sample rescue report is included in appendix B.

We've discussed the various methods for using a rescue tube to rescue someone. But what should you do if you lose control of your rescue tube or a struggling person grabs you instead of the rescue tube for support? Let's discuss techniques for escaping from someone's grasp.

Emergency Escape

A person who is struggling in the water and grabs you instead of a rescue tube or other means of flotation has one objective in mind: to stay on the surface. If you realize that you are about to be grabbed, try to get a quick breath of air and position your head so that you will not be choked if someone grabs your head. Use the phrase "suck, tuck, and duck" to remind you to suck in a breath of air, tuck your chin, and try to duck away from the person's grasp.

If a struggling person does grasp you around your head, submerge under the water, taking the person with you. Often, that action will cause the person to release you, because his or her objective is to remain on the surface. If the person does not release you, follow these steps to perform an emergency escape:

1. Place your hands under the person's upper arms and push firmly up and away.

2. If you are not released, place your hands on the person's hips and press him or her away from you while you duck out from the grasp.

3. When you are free of the person's grasp, quickly move backward out of reach.

4. Surface, reposition your rescue tube, and attempt the rescue again.

Seizures in the Water

If a patron experiences a seizure while in the water, he or she may not have the body control to be able to keep the head above water and breathe. The behaviors associated with seizures range from very subtle changes in responsiveness to evident convulsions. A person having a convulsion may be jerking uncontrollably, with random arm and leg movements. A seizure usually lasts only a minute or so, followed by several minutes of recovery when the person may still be somewhat unresponsive.

When a seizure occurs in the water, the primary goal is to keep the person's head above water to reduce the chance of swallowing water or allowing water to obstruct the airway. This goal is easily achieved by holding the seizing person's head above water. If possible, you may want to place a rescue tube under the person, but you do not want to try to grab around a person having a seizure, such as you would in a rear rescue. Rather, hold the head in a position above the water first, and then place the rescue tube under the person if possible or if needed.

If the seizing person can be safely extricated while the convulsions are occurring, consider doing so and continue with care on deck. You should also extricate immediately if you cannot keep the person's head above water. Otherwise, remove the person from the water after the seizure stops.

StarGuard Performance Goal

When managing a distressed swimmer or drowning victim, follow the Starfish Aquatic Rescue Model:

1. Scan.
2. Target.
3. Assess.
4. Alert.
5. Rescue.

StarGuard Best Practices

- Help a distressed person within reach by extending a rescue tube.
- Use a rescue tube for all water rescues in order to avoid your upper body contacting the victim's upper body.
- Provide safety instructions to a rescued person.
- Suck, tuck, and duck to keep from being grabbed in the water.
- Complete a report for all rescues.

Managing Aquatic Spinal Injuries

Spinal injuries do not occur in the water unless some sort of trauma causes the injury. Spinal injuries can result if a person strikes his or her head, neck, or back. In an aquatic environment this trauma can come from hitting the wall, the diving board, a starting block, another person, or the bottom. These events are called mechanism of injury.

When managing a spinal injury in the water, you must do two things differently than if you were on land. First, if the injured person is facedown, turn the person over so that he or she can breathe, while at the same time minimizing the movement of the person's head, neck, and spine to prevent further injury. This technique is called in-line stabilization. Second, the injured person must be removed from the water. A backboard can be used to further minimize movement during this process. Your facility's emergency action plan (EAP) and protocol for suspected spinal injuries should specify whether lifeguards or EMS personnel perform backboarding. Before rescuing a person in the water who may have a spinal injury, follow the STAAR protocol:

- Scan. You scan your zone.
- Target. If you see something happen that could cause a spinal injury or recognize symptoms of a spinal injury, target on the person.
- Assess. You should suspect a spinal injury if you see something that could cause an injury. Decide to take action.
- Alert. You activate your facility EAP for spinal injury.

- Rescue. If you are within a few feet of the person, you use an ease-in entry so that you do not create excessive water movement around the injured person.

In-Line Stabilization

If a person with a suspected spinal injury is in the water, your first step is to provide in-line stabilization. The objectives are as follows:

- Minimize movement of the head, neck, and spine.
- Keep the person's head above water so that he or she can breathe.
- Move to shallow water or a takeout point and prepare to place the injured person on a backboard or wait for EMS, depending on the guidelines established with your EMS provider.

The best technique you use to provide in-line stabilization depends on whether the person is faceup or facedown, is on the surface or submerged, is in shallow water or deep water, and possibly, on the person's size or shoulder flexibility. In-line stabilization techniques in the water include the vise grip (if a person is faceup), vise-grip rollover (if a person is facedown), ease-up to vise grip (if a person is submerged), and the spinal rollover (if the person has limited shoulder flexibility).

Vise Grip

Perform a vise grip if a person with a suspected spinal injury is faceup in either shallow or deep water. Follow these steps to stabilize the person:

Approach the person at their feet and position yourself next to the person. In deep water, position your rescue tube low on your hips; in shallow water the rescue tube may not be necessary.

Reach over the person and place your hands on his or her upper arms between the elbows and shoulders. Press the person's arms into his or her head to form a "vise" to minimize movement. Once you make contact and squeeze the arms to the head, do not let go or readjust your hand position.

3 Proceed to the takeout point, preferably in shallow water.

Vise-Grip Rollover

If a person with a suspected spinal injury is facedown in the water, paralysis may prevent him or her from being able to roll over or lift the head to breath. Your objective will be to roll him or her over as quickly as possible while minimizing the movement of the head, neck, and spine. As long as the head is submerged the person cannot breathe and is a drowning victim, so time is of the essence. Follow these steps to perform a vise-grip rollover:

Approach the person at their feet and position yourself next to the person. In deep water, position your rescue tube low on your hips; in shallow water the rescue tube may not be necessary.

Reach over the person and place your hands on his or her upper arms between the elbows and shoulders. Press the person's arms into his or her head to form a "vise" to minimize movement. Once you make contact and squeeze the arms to the head, do not let go or readjust your hand position.

Roll the person over slowly, keeping pressure on his or her arms. Move forward only if momentum is needed to execute the roll or if you need to move the person into a horizontal position. At this point you do not know if the person's mouth is open or closed and forward movement could cause the person to swallow water.

4 Move to the takeout point, preferably in shallow water. Talk to the person to check his or her level of consciousness. Wait for EMS or prepare to place the person on a backboard, depending on the procedures at your facility.

Alternative Vise-Grip Rollover

This technique is best for situations in which you will backboard shortly after the rollover. The water should be shallow enough for you to stand. You roll the person away from you, which keeps your arm from being under the person and eliminates the extra step of having to remove it before backboarding. Follow these steps to perform an alternative vise-grip rollover:

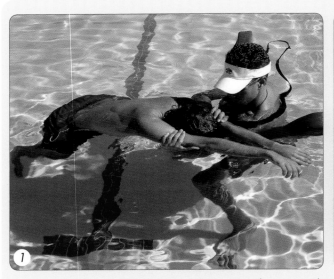

Position yourself next to the person. With your outside arm, reach under the person and grasp his or her outside arm between the elbow and shoulder. Place your hand that is closest to the person on his or her arm between the elbow and the shoulder. Press the person's arms into his or her head to form a "vise" to minimize movement.

Roll the person over slowly away from you by initiating the roll with the hand closest to your body. Keep pressure on the person's arms.

Move to the takeout point, preferably in shallow water and backboard. Talk to the person to check his or her level of consciousness.

Ease-Up to Vise Grip

If a person is submerged deeper than your reach, you must slowly ease the person up toward the surface without causing unnatural movement of the head, neck, or spine. As long as a person is submerged, the weightlessness of the water keeps the head and neck in a neutral, nonmoving position and the surrounding properties of the water cushion and support the head and neck. The first objective of the ease-up technique is to make just enough contact with the injured person to initiate a weightless rise to the surface. The second objective is to position a rescue tube so that as soon as the person is near the surface and within reach, you can initiate a vise grip in a smooth transition. This transition eliminates the bouncing and bobbing at the surface that is common with other techniques, and it can be performed by one rescuer. Follow these steps to perform an ease-up to vise grip:

Position yourself above and behind the person. Maintain contact with your rescue tube and extend your body, feetfirst, toward the person.

Secure the person with your legs just under his or her armpits. Make just enough contact to initiate a rise to the surface.

As he or she begins to rise to the surface, release your legs and move away from the person. Position yourself to perform a vise grip or vise-grip rollover (if the person is face down). Talk to the person to check his or her level of consciousness.

Spinal Rollover

In some instances, a person's body size or flexibility will not allow his or her arms to come together enough to form a vise grip around the head. In this case, a front-to-back stabilization method minimizes the movement of the head, neck, and spine. You can perform this technique on a person standing or lying in the water either faceup or facedown. If the person is facedown, she or he must be rolled over to be able to breathe. Follow these steps to perform a spinal rollover:

At the same time, place one of your hands on the back of the person's head, with your arm down along the spine. Gently move the person's arm that is closest to you down toward the person's side.

Place the fingers of your other hand on his or her cheekbones, with your arm down along the person's chest. Maintain even pressure from the front and back and be sure you are not covering the person's mouth with your hand. To roll the person, submerge yourself and rise on the other side. The objective of the spinal rollover is to have one of your arms along the person's spine and your other arm along the person's chest. Depending on the person's size, it may be necessary to first gently move the person's arm closest to you down, allowing you to obtain the best stabilizing position.

After you have used one of these techniques for in-line stabilization in the water, you should monitor the injured person's airway, breathing, and circulation (ABCs) and try to keep the person as warm as possible to prevent hypothermia until EMS arrives, or you should backboard and extricate according to your facility's protocol.

Backboarding Equipment

Backboarding is a site-specific technique, dependent on the type of equipment available, water depth, amount of rescuers present, deck and gutter configuration, and other considerations. Backboarding equipment consists of three components: the backboard, the head immobilization device, and the body straps.

Backboards are made out of wood or molded plastic. A backboard suitable for extrication from the water should have numerous handholds at both ends and along the sides. It is also important that the backboard have runners on the bottom or be molded in a way that will keep your fingers away from under the board when it is flat against the deck. Runners will also allow you to slide, rather than lift, the board out of the pool and onto the deck, reducing your chance of injury.

A head immobilization device (HID) attaches to the backboard at the place where the injured person's head will be located when placed on the backboard. The purpose of the HID is to keep the injured person's head, neck, and spine in line and prevent movement in instances where manual stabilization cannot be provided. The method by which the HID attaches to the backboard, and the techniques for applying the devices to an injured person's head vary widely depending on the type of device.

A backboard must have some means of securing an injured person and should be fitted with several body straps. The two most common types of straps are wide strips of Velcro that close up on themselves across the person and thick straps made of webbing with a plastic snap-in clip or seatbelt-style buckle. Some strapping systems are applied straight across. Others crisscross, and some expand from a central point in a "spider" method. Straps that are color-coded will help you locate the match more easily in the water. In most circumstances, a backboard with five body straps is sufficient. However, if the pool deck or gutter is much higher than the surface of the water, you may

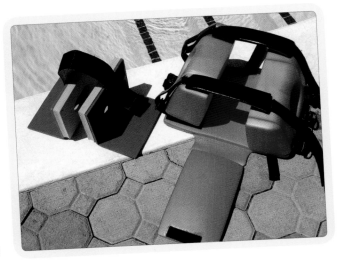

need to place the injured person in an almost vertical position during extrication. In this event, you may need additional straps under the person's feet to keep him or her from sliding down.

Preparing to Backboard

If a person with a suspected spinal injury is in the water, at some point he or she will need to be removed from the water, which is also called extrication. A backboard is usually used for this purpose. It is important to know, practice, and follow the backboarding and extrication protocol established for your facility, which should be determined together with your local EMS. The 2005 first aid guidelines recommend that first aid providers restrict spinal motion by manual stabilization, rather than by using devices. Whenever possible, you should provide manual stabilization of the head and neck during backboarding and extrication, which requires a minimum of three rescuers.

In instances where it is not feasible to use manual stabilization during backboarding and extrication, such as when only two rescuers are present, you will need to use a HID to stabilize the person's head and neck while you and the other rescuer(s) remove the person from the water. If the person has altered levels of consciousness, reestablish manual stabilization and remove the HID so you are prepared to provide airway management if rescue breathing or CPR are needed.

Change-Up

If you are going to backboard and extricate an injured person from the water, you must perform a change-up to move your arm from under the person so that you can place him or her on a backboard. Follow these steps to perform a change-up:

While in the vise-grip position, apply pressure with your outer hand to squeeze the person to your chest.

2 When he or she is tight against your chest, release the grasp of your hand that is closest to your chest, reach over the person, and place the hand next to your other one.

Keep squeezing the person's body to your chest and slide your arm that is under the person toward your body. Make contact with the person's upper arm, and apply pressure. When you are applying even pressure to the person's arms with both of your hands, move him or her away from your chest.

Backboarding and Extrication Objectives

This course teaches you the objectives for backboarding, which remain the same regardless of the type of facility, equipment, or number of rescuers or bystanders available to help. In chronological sequence, the objectives for backboarding include the following:

1. Minimize water movement around the person during your entry.
2. Provide in-line stabilization; roll the person over if he or she is facedown.
3. Monitor the person's airway, breathing, and circulation; if needed, provide basic life support. Use a modified jaw thrust if the airway must be opened.

4. Place the backboard under or behind the person while stabilizing his or her head and neck.

5. Strap the person's body to the board, starting at the chest and then down to the feet.

6. Maintain in-line stabilization and immobilize the head.

7. Check the security of the body straps and adjust them. Strap in the persons hands if necessary to prevent injury during extrication.

8. Extricate the person.

9. Keep the person warm and monitor ABCs until EMS arrives. Apply emergency oxygen, if available.

To illustrate how you might achieve these backboarding objectives in different circumstances, let's look at the steps involved when two lifeguards backboard a person in deep water, when several lifeguards backboard someone in shallow water, and when three lifeguards perform a standing takedown in a slide-catch pool. But keep in mind that these descriptions are intended to illustrate backboarding objectives, not rescue procedures. The specific procedure in place at the facility where you work may be different. If your employer will require you to backboard people with suspected spinal injuries, you must receive additional training using the equipment at the facility where you work.

Two-Guard Backboarding

This two-guard backboarding scenario involves an initial rescuer in the water and a backup rescuer on the deck. The initial rescuer began the sequence with the steps of the STAAR Aquatic Rescue Model and performed an ease-in entry to minimize water movement around the injured person.

1 The initial rescuer signals for help and for a backboard before making contact with the injured person. The backup rescuer brings the backboard to the scene and puts on gloves in case bodily fluids are present during care.

The initial rescuer provides in-water stabilization and starts moving the person toward the backboard. The backup rescuer grasps the handholds at the top of the backboard and places the board vertically in the water as deep as possible, pressing the bottom of the board against the pool wall to keep it from moving.

The initial rescuer lines up the injured person with the backboard and moves in slowly toward the wall. The backup rescuer positions the backboard to allow it to raise up under the injured person. The goal is to place the person's head on the HID mounting area.

(continued)

(continued)

The backup rescuer kneels or lies down on the deck and stabilizes the board with her elbows. With the hands and forearms, she takes control of maintaining the stabilization of the person's head from the initial rescuer.

The initial rescuer first straps the person's chest then the rest of the body, while the backup rescuer maintains control of the head.

The initial rescuer takes over control of the person's head by placing his fingers on the person's cheekbones and his forearm along the person's chest. He places his other arm under the backboard and presses upward for support.

The backup rescuer places both HID pieces at the same time and then applies the head strap. The backup rescuer maintains contact with the backboard and monitors the person's condition.

The initial rescuer checks the body straps and adjusts them if necessary; he may need to strap the person's hands to avoid injury during extrication. The initial rescuer climbs out and, on count, both rescuers slide the backboard up and out of the pool using the runners, rather than lifting. One of the rescuers keeps the person warm, monitors her condition until EMS arrives, and applies emergency oxygen, if available.

Team Backboarding

This team backboarding scenario involves an initial rescuer and several backup rescuers. The initial rescuer began the sequence with the steps of the STAAR Aquatic Rescue Model and performed an ease-in entry to minimize water movement around the injured person.

The initial rescuer signals for help and calls for a backboard before making contact with the injured person. The backup rescuers bring the backboard and place it in the water. The initial rescuer provides in-water stabilization. The backup rescuers place the backboard parallel to the injured person.

The backup rescuers lift the side of the backboard at an angle then press the board down and under the person.

The injured person's head should be on the HID mounting area with one rescuer positioned at the head of the board and another rescuer at the foot of the board.

The rescuer at the top of the board takes control of in-line stabilization of the head from the initial rescuer. The initial rescuer then applies the body straps starting with the chest, followed by the rest of the body. The rescuer at the foot helps stabilize the board.

(continued)

(continued)

When strapping is complete, the initial rescuer takes control of the person's head by placing his fingers on her cheekbones and his forearm along her chest. He places his other arm under the backboard and presses upward for support. The rescuer at the head of the board places both of the HID pieces at the same time, then applies the head strap.

The initial rescuer checks the body straps and adjusts them if necessary, and may strap the person's hands to avoid injury during extrication. The rescuer at the head climbs out onto the deck, and lifts the board above the pool edge. The other rescuers position themselves at the foot of the backboard and help slide the board onto the deck. The rescuers keep the person warm, monitor her condition until EMS arrives, and apply emergency oxygen if available.

In-Water Standing Takedown

This in-water standing takedown scenario involves an initial rescuer and two backup rescuers. The initial rescuer began the sequence with the steps of the STAAR Aquatic Rescue Model and performed an ease-in entry to minimize water movement around the injured person.

1 The initial rescuer signals for help and calls for a backboard before making contact with the injured person. The backup rescuers bring the backboard and enter the water.

The initial rescuer minimizes movement of the person's head by placing his open hands on either side of his head and extending his arms down the person's chest. He positions himself slightly off center in case the person vomits. The backup rescuers place the backboard behind the person.

The backup rescuers secure the person to the backboard by reaching under his armpit and grasping the backboard handhold. The initial rescuer maintains control of the person's head.

One of the backup rescuers takes over control of the person's head by placing the fingers of his free hand between those of the initial rescuer. As the backup rescuer begins to apply even pressure, the initial rescuer slides his hands down and out.

The initial rescuer moves to the back of the backboard and grasps the top of the board by the handhold. On his count, all rescuers lower the backboard slowly to a horizontal position while maintaining even pressure against the person's head.

If necessary, reposition the backboard so that the person's head is on the HID mounting area. Submerge the backboard slightly and move it in the direction of the person's feet about three inches at a time.

The initial rescuer takes control of the person's head. From a position at the top of the backboard, he slides his fingers and palms under the person's shoulders and places his thumbs over the person's shoulders. He then slides his forearms along the person's head, applying even pressure as the backup rescuers move their hands.

The backup rescuers first strap the chest then the rest of the body. One of the backup rescuers takes over control of the person's head by placing his fingers on the person's cheekbones and his forearm along the person's chest. Another rescuer places both HID pieces at the same time and then applies the head strap.

The rescuers check the body straps and adjust them if necessary. They may need to strap the person's hands to avoid injury during extrication.

(continued)

(continued)

The rescuers position themselves with one at the head and the others on each side, all grasping the handholds. They carry the injured person up the pool steps, or lift the board until the backboard is even with the deck; they then use the backboard runners to slide the backboard out of the pool. One of the rescuers keeps the person warm, monitors his condition until EMS arrives, and applies emergency oxygen if available.

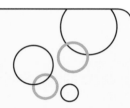

StarGuard Performance Goal

If in-water spinal injury is suspected, provide in-line stabilization and monitor the person's airway until EMS arrives. If local protocol indicates, backboard and extricate the person while minimizing movement of the head, neck, and spine.

StarGuard Best Practices

- Suspect spinal injury if you know a mechanism of injury is present.
- Know the spinal-injury protocol for your facility.
- Practice spinal-injury management with the equipment at your facility.

Managing an Unconscious Drowning Victim

Your goal in managing an unconscious, nonbreathing drowning victim is simple: Obtain an unobstructed, open airway as quickly as possible so that the drowning victim can start spontaneous breathing or so that you can begin emergency care. The key words in this statement are *unobstructed* and *quickly*. This chapter prepares you to begin airway management while you are still in the water so that the drowning victim has the best chance of becoming a drowning survivor. The chapter also explains the best way to remove an unconscious victim who does not have a spinal injury from the water.

Water Rescue

If a drowning victim is not breathing and it is likely to take longer than 30 seconds to remove the person from the water, begin care in the water by opening the airway and following the guidelines for providing emergency care for victims who are not breathing. If you are very close to a takeout point and you can remove the person from the water in 30 seconds or less, wait to begin emergency care and basic life support on land. Circumstances during the emergency, including the distance between the drowning victim and the takeout point, will determine which technique you should use. The objective is to circulate blood to the organs as quickly as possible, open the airway, clear any obstructions, and give the victim oxygen.

Having a rescue tube and barrier mask immediately available is critical to your success in rescuing an unconscious drowning victim. The mask should be capable of making a reasonable seal in the water, and the one-way valve should be made of plastic or a nonabsorbent material (not paper or fiber). The mask must be easily accessible, for instance, kept in a pack either around your waist or attached to your rescue tube.

When you use a rescue tube to perform a rear rescue on an unconscious drowning victim, you are in an excellent position to provide immediate emergency care. When you place a drowning victim on the rescue tube, his or her head will fall back into an open-airway position. From this position behind the person's head, you can place the mask and begin rescue breathing and still be able to swim and progress toward a takeout point. Providing ventilation immediately, while you're still in the water, can be crucial to a successful rescue outcome—especially when you are not sure how long a drowning victim has been submerged and without oxygen. Let's look at how to perform this technique in more detail.

Emergency Care in the Water

If your takeout point is more than about 20 feet (6 meters) away or removal from the water is likely to take longer than 30 seconds, begin rescue breathing in the water. Follow these steps to perform rescue breathing in the water:

Follow the STAAR rescue model: scan, target, assess, alert, rescue. When you reach the drowning victim, place him or her on the rescue tube, using either a rear rescue or leg-wrap rescue if the person is submerged. If the drowning victim does not begin to cough, move, or show signs of breathing when you lift his or her face out of the water, raise your fist to signal that you need help.

Obtain your pocket mask. From a position behind the drowning victim's head, place the pocket mask over the person's nose and mouth. Make a good seal. Give two slow breaths, followed by additional breaths at the rate determined by the emergency cardiac care guidelines to be appropriate for the age and size of the drowning victim.

(continued)

3

Keep moving the drowning victim toward the takeout point as you continue rescue breathing. Once you have reached the side of the pool, you must remove the person from the water and place him or her on the deck so that you can continue basic life support care until EMS arrives.

Extrication

Your objective when removing an unconscious drowning victim (who does not have a suspected spinal injury) from the water is to do so as quickly as possible and in a way that minimizes the risk of injury to you or the drowning victim. Factors that may affect the type of removal method you choose include the following:

- Size of the deck and gutter. Extrication is much easier if the water and deck are at nearly the same level.
- Size of the drowning victim. You may not need a removal device to lift a small person out of the water.
- Available equipment. A backboard (without using the HID or straps) is ideal for quick extrication.
- Number of people available to assist. Use several helpers if they're available, especially when removing a large or heavy person from the water.

Practice various methods of extrication at the facility where you work, using the equipment available. This practice will help you determine which techniques—the backboard pullout, the backboard walkout, or an alternate method—are effective in meeting the objectives for extrication. Remember, the objective is to remove the person as quickly as possible with the least chance of injury to either the victim or the rescuers.

Backboard Pullout

A backboard, found at most aquatic facilities, is very useful in removing a person quickly from the water. When using a backboard to remove an unconscious drowning victim who is not suspected of having a spinal injury, you don't need to place the headpieces or straps. Follow these steps to perform a backboard pullout:

As the first rescuer approaches the takeout point with the drowning victim, the second rescuer places the backboard vertically in the water.

When within the second rescuer's reach, the first rescuer lifts the drowning victim's arm up to the second rescuer then pulls the rescue tube out from under the victim. The second rescuer holds the victim's arm with one hand and the top of the board with the other.

When the victim is secure, the second rescuer tilts the board back so that it is in a seesaw position on the edge of the pool. The first rescuer either moves to the end of the board to help push or climbs out and helps pull.

The second rescuer gives the count then tilts the head of the board back while sliding and pulling the board up and out onto the deck. He or she continues pulling until the victim is several feet away from the pool edge and out of standing water, as illustrated, in case an automated external defibrillator (AED) will be used.

Backboard Walkout

Use a backboard walkout extrication where the water is shallow and there are wide stairs or a zero-depth area. This extrication requires at least four rescuers and more if the drowning victim is large or heavy. Follow these steps to perform a backboard walkout:

1. Submerge the backboard and slide it under the drowning victim.
2. Strap his or her chest to the backboard.
3. Rescuers position themselves evenly around the board, with at least two on each side, and grasp the handholds.
4. Float the board until the water is so shallow that it can no longer float. The rescuers then lift and support the board as they walk out of the zero-depth area or up the stairs.

Once the unconscious drowning victim is out of the water and on the deck or shore, immediately begin or resume providing emergency care. Be prepared to provide basic life support and, if available, integrate additional rescue equipment such as emergency oxygen or an Automated External Defibrillator (AED) into your efforts and then to transfer care of the person to EMS when they arrive.

Special Considerations for Providing Basic Life Support

Note: This section is to be supplemented with American Safety and Health Institute (ASHI) CPR course for professional rescuers.

When caring for an unconscious drowning victim, you will use the techniques you learned during your ASHI CPR training for professional rescuers. However, you may need to modify these techniques somewhat because the person you are rescuing has been submerged in water and without air for (usually) an unknown amount of time. The following situations may occur when rescuing an unconscious drowning victim:

- The person may have swallowed large quantities of water, making a large swollen stomach common and vomiting highly likely. Foam and mucus are also likely to come out of the mouth and nose of an unconscious drowning victim. These circumstances may make it difficult for you to obtain or maintain an open airway. You will need to be prepared to clear the airway of vomit, mucus, or other fluids to maintain an open airway. Use the techniques you learned in your emergency care training.
- The person may make gasping or snoring sounds that you might mistake for attempts to breathe. However, these sounds are caused by changes occurring in the body and are called agonal breathing. If 10 or more seconds pass between these sounds, continue or start CPR.
- Because you and the drowning victim will both be wet and possibly cold and you may be breathing heavily from executing the rescue, it will be difficult for you to effectively check the victim's pulse. If possible, have another rescuer

check the pulse, or rely on the signs-of-circulation method to determine when to start CPR.

- Your hands may be wet, and you need to be prepared to begin basic life support care immediately after removing the drowning victim from the water. Practice putting latex or silicone gloves on your wet hands, using the technique of filling the gloves with water first (see page 20) to save valuable time. Rescuers who come to assist should put on gloves while moving toward the scene, so they don't delay care while putting on their gloves.

- Because the drowning victim will likely be wearing a swimsuit, you should be able to easily see the person's nipple line. Use this visual reference to quickly locate the correct hand position (on the sternum between the nipples) for CPR compressions.

Integrating Adjunct Equipment

Although bag-valve masks (BVM), manual suction devices, emergency oxygen, and automated external defibrillators can enhance the care you provide, your critical focus should be on providing basic life support care and monitoring the person's airway, breathing, and circulation (ABCs). If your facility provides adjunct equipment, backup rescuers will most likely have to bring it to the scene, so there could be a delay from the time you are ready to begin care and when the equipment arrives. You can integrate this equipment into your resuscitation efforts at any time in the following ways:

- There may be water on the deck near the edge of the pool. If you will use an AED, extricate the unconscious drowning victim to a position at least 6 feet (2 meters) away from the pool edge (if deck space permits) in order to reduce the amount of water surrounding the rescue scene.

- When someone brings an AED to the scene, immediately turn on the unit and apply the pads to the victim's bare chest. Be sure the chest is as dry as possible. The drowning victim's chest will be wet. Keep a small towel with your AED so that you can dry the chest before applying the pads so that they will stick.

- The scene will be noisy, and acoustics in an aquatic facility may be bad. Have a designated rescuer or bystander listen closely to the AED prompts and call out the commands.

- If you will use emergency oxygen, keep the cylinder in the bag or case—not on the slippery deck—so that it does not get knocked over.

- If a bag-valve mask is not available, begin providing ventilations using your pocket mask. Have another rescuer prepare the BVM and hand it to you when it is ready. You should maintain control of the person's airway, and the other rescuer should squeeze the bag to provide ventilations.

- When someone brings a manual suction device to the scene, have another rescuer prepare the device (some have a cap that must be removed or a tube that must be attached) and place it in the ready position. Ideally, the rescuer responsible for suctioning and the suctioning devise will be located on one side of the victim, with the other equipment, such as oxygen or AED, on the other side. This prevents vomit or other fluids from getting on the other equipment.

- When someone brings emergency oxygen to the scene, have another rescuer prepare the mask and tubing and turn on the flow. The rescuer should tell you "oxygen is flowing" after verifying that the unit is on. You can either switch masks or, if your mask has an oxygen intake port, attach the tubing to the mask you are already using.

Do not wait for additional (adjunct) equipment before you begin care. Integrate these items as other rescuers bring them to the scene.

Transferring to EMS

When EMS personnel arrive at the site, have a staff person direct them to the rescue scene. Once they arrive, it is likely that they will tell you to continue your resuscitation efforts as they set up equipment and prepare to take over care. During this transition, follow the directives the EMTs or paramedics give you and be prepared to answer questions about the drowning victim's condition, length of time unconscious, and other symptoms or circumstances. Someone on your rescue team (usually the supervisor) should do the following:

- Make a note of the EMS arrival time.
- Find out which hospital the drowning victim will be transported to.
- Make a note of the responding EMS unit and the names of the EMS personnel.
- Obtain replacement equipment from the EMS vehicle if they are taking your equipment (e.g., backboard).

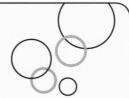

StarGuard Performance Goal

When managing an unconscious, nonbreathing drowning victim, obtain an unobstructed, open airway as quickly as possible and attempt to ventilate within 30 seconds of contact. After extrication, begin care then integrate adjunct equipment if and when it arrives on the scene.

StarGuard Best Practices

- Have a pocket mask available to you in the water.
- Extricate an unconscious person using a backboard as a pullout device.
- Pull out at least 6 feet (2 meters) from the pool edge if deck space permits.
- Back-up rescuers should glove up on the way to the scene to save time.
- Keep emergency oxygen in the bag or case.
- Have a towel available to dry a person's chest before applying AED pads.

Professionalism and Personal Safety

Objectives

Knowledge	Skill	Execution
After reading part V, you should understand the following:	After instructor-observed practice, you should be able to perform the following:	After scenario and site-specific training, you should be able to do the following:
The facts about skin cancer and your skin cancer risks The need for skin and eye protection to reduce exposure to the sun The considerations for safe practices in the workplace The importance of maintaining physical fitness The importance of maintaining good vision and obtaining eye exams The risks of personal injury or illness to lifeguards posed by biohazards and response to emergencies The risks of emotional distress to lifeguards posed by responding to emergencies or being involved in a lawsuit The factors that create or take away from a professional image The importance of in-service (enrichment) training The need for accountability and the importance of lifeguard performance audits The general principles of legal liability and negligence related to lifeguarding The need to use sound judgment when making decisions, even after hours The situations that create difficult working environments for lifeguards How to help people with disabilities enjoy aquatic recreation with dignity The equipment, training, and support that your employer should provide		Perform lifeguard duties based on the StarGuard best practices, while maintaining your health and safety.

Personal Health and Safety

Although your focus as a lifeguard is on the safety of patrons, your personal safety in and around an aquatic environment is also important. You are exposed to the same risks as the patrons who use your facility but at a much higher frequency. This chapter provides information to help you manage some of the workplace safety risks of your profession: sun exposure, workplace dangers, injury during rescues, illness caused by the environment, and emotional problems that may result from rescue attempts.

Skin Cancer Awareness

The sun is the primary cause of skin cancer, and chronic exposure to the sun's ultraviolet rays is the most significant risk factor for developing all types of skin cancer. If you work outdoors, you are at risk. The good news is that skin cancer is preventable, but before we talk about protection and screening, here are some sobering facts from the Skin Cancer Foundation:

- Skin cancer is the most common form of cancer in the United States. More than one million skin cancers are diagnosed annually.
- One in five Americans will develop skin cancer in the course of a lifetime.
- Up to 90 percent of the visible changes commonly attributed to aging are caused by the sun.
- More than 20 Americans die each day from skin cancer, primarily melanoma. One person dies of melanoma almost every hour (every 62 minutes).

- Melanoma is the second most common form of cancer for young adults 15-29 years old.
- One or more blistering sunburns in childhood or adolescence more than double a person's changes of developing melanoma later in life.
- A person's risk for melanoma doubles if he or she has had more than five sunburns at any age.
- The incidence of many common cancers is falling, but the incidence of melanoma continues to rise significantly, at a rate faster than that of any of the seven most common cancers.

Information courtesy of The Skin Cancer Foundation, New York. www.skincancer.org.

Your lifeguarding job should not be an excuse to get a suntan. You must take personal responsibility to protect yourself, and the best way to accomplish this is to use skin protection products and to cover up.

- *Always* use sunscreen and lip coat rated at SPF 15 or higher. Apply sunscreen at least 30 minutes before exposure. A sunscreen log for documenting application should be used by the lifeguard staff (an example is shown on page 114).
- In addition to sunscreen, use sun shade. Have at least one physical barrier, such as a hat, shirt, or umbrella, between you and the sun.
- Examine your skin regularly, and seek a physician's opinion if you have suspicious-looking moles or dark areas on your skin.

Workplace Safety

Your employer is required by law to provide a safe working environment. But just as patrons must share in the responsibility for their own safety, you must also share in the responsibility for your safety. Follow these tips to avoid work-related injury:

- If you must handle chemicals or hazardous materials, follow the established guidelines and precautions as detailed in the material safety data sheets (MSDS) your employer will provide you. You have a legal right to know about any risks associated with chemical products, and the MSDS provides this information. In addition, your employer should provide training for safe handling of these chemicals and hazardous materials. Your employer may use an MSDS literature station to display this information.
- Know and practice the emergency action plans at your facility for fires, emergency evacuation, procedures for performing rescues or first aid duties, and alarm system requirements.

- Take care when climbing in or out of lifeguard chairs that are wet or slippery.
- Walk, don't run, on the pool deck—even during emergencies. You cannot provide care to someone else if you are injured on the way to the scene.
- Keep floors cleared of obstructions, and keep guardrails and covers to pits or vats in place.
- When possible, avoid closing or opening your facility when you are alone. If you are alone, consider carrying a cell phone or a personal defense device such as pepper spray and have your whistle ready in case you need to signal for help.
- Follow all the rules and policies of your facility at all times, even when you are using the facility for after-hours training or staff events.
- If you work outdoors, carry insect repellant.
- Obtain practical (hands-on) instruction for or equipment you will be authorized to use such a pool vacuum, lawn tools, or motor-powered watercraft.
- Notify your supervisor immediately or call 9-1-1 if a patron physically threatens you or if violent behavior breaks out or appears likely at your facility.

Physical Fitness

It is your responsibility to minimize your risk of being injured during a rescue. The best way to reduce this risk is to maintain your rescue skills and stay in reasonable physical condition. An effective physical fitness program should include at least 30 minutes of exercise (e.g., swimming, running, weight training, cycling) at least five times per week.

One way to motivate yourself to exercise may be to work out with your coworkers. Regularly scheduled runs, rides, or swims can help you plan ahead and keep you focused on your fitness goals. The key to improving your fitness level is finding an activity and a workout group that you enjoy so that you will exercise consistently.

Medical Considerations

One of your most important lifeguarding tools is your eyes. Most of your time is spent using them to scan for visual indications of problems. Adequate eyesight is critical to your success. Follow these tips to protect your vision:

- Shield your eyes from the effects of the sun, wind, water, and dust by wearing sunglasses that are both 100 percent ultraviolet protective and physically protective.
- Labels on sunglasses may be misleading. Look for the words "ANSI standards" or "UV protection up to 400nm" to be sure the lenses filter 100 percent of UV rays.
- Have your eyes tested at least once a year to screen for vision problems.
- If you wear glasses or contact lenses to correct your vision, wear them at all times when you are on duty.

- If you wear contact lenses, close your eyes briefly when you enter the water in order to avoid losing your lenses. If you know you will be swimming with lenses in or may have to get in the water during a rescue, consider wearing disposable lenses so that if the lenses do come out, they are easily replaced.

- Keep your lenses clean and replace them as needed. Chlorine and other pool contaminants may remain in a contact lens and cause eye inflammation.

Information courtesy of Park District Risk Management Agency (PDRMA).

Other methods to reduce work-related illness include the following:

- Minimize your risk of dehydration, heat exhaustion, or heatstroke by drinking lots of water. Keep a water bottle on the stand and make sure you have protection from the sun.

- Obtain a hepatitis B vaccination if you have not been immunized.

- Do not swallow recreational water.

- Always use your personal protective equipment when cleaning up bodily substances.

- Remove wet swimwear frequently to avoid skin chafing and urinary tract infections.

- Wear sandals to prevent exposure to fungus or bacteria and to protect feet from cuts.

Emotional Health

Although you encounter physical risks while lifeguarding, the risk to your emotional health caused by the stress of responding to emergencies may be even greater. The best way to remain emotionally healthy and able to manage the day-to-day stresses of lifeguarding is to use common sense, know established procedures, and practice your skills often. However, if a traumatic incident does occur at your facility, you may find it difficult to deal with the long-term psychological effects of this event.

If you witness a drowning at your facility, whether the drowning victim was a survivor or a fatality, you must take care of yourself and your coworkers both physically and emotionally after the incident. The anxiety and stress associated with a drowning will continue for a long time, especially if a lawsuit is filed. It is likely that you will be questioned numerous times about the incident—by the police, representatives from the insurance company, attorneys, your supervisors, and others. The following are strategies to help you cope:

- As soon as possible after the incident, relieve the stress by getting physically active. Go for a swim, run, or do another workout activity.
- Get back to your regular patterns of work, school, and social events. The familiarity of day-to-day activities will provide stability in your life.
- Take advantage of the debriefing sessions your facility may schedule to deal with critical-incident stress. These sessions usually will be conducted for your benefit within a few days of the incident. Mental health care professionals trained to help emergency care workers deal with stress after a traumatic event will facilitate these group discussions.
- When you start to feel overwhelmed, talk to friends or relatives close to you who will be supportive without being judgmental.

StarGuard Performance Goal

Minimize your risk of illness or injury while on duty so you can perform at your best.

StarGuard Best Practices

- Shade yourself from the sun with a shirt, hat, umbrella, or all three.
- Apply sunscreen with an SPF value of at least 15.
- Wear sunglasses during daylight hours.
- Stay hydrated by drinking water.
- Exercise to maintain fitness.

Sunscreen Log

Name	Date	Time	SPF applied

From *StarGuard: Best Practices for Lifeguards, Third Edition* by Jill E. White, 2006, Champaign, IL: Human Kinetics.

13

Professionalism

Professionalism is one of the most important components of the StarGuard course because it carries through to everything you do. This chapter explains the various components of professionalism and how these traits relate to your performance as a lifeguard, including image, demeanor, commitment to improvement, accountability, communication, and the ability to make sound decisions, especially in difficult situations. Being professional also means knowing how to relate to different types of individuals, including those with special physical or medical needs. You must understand the legal risks to which you may be exposed and, in all circumstances, you need to know the types of support necessary from your employer to be able to meet the expectations of your job.

Projecting a Professional Image

Professionalism can be expressed in many ways; the most common is the opinion that others have of you based on the way you act, talk, dress, or perform your duties. Even something as simple as the way you sit in the lifeguard stand can affect the professional image you project. Note the differences in the photos on page 116 between a very professional posture and a less professional posture.

To perform your job at a high level, you must instill confidence in the patrons you serve. Because they may not know anything about you, the only way they can evaluate your ability is through what they see. If you slouch in the lifeguard stand looking bored and twirling your whistle, they will assume that you are bored and don't care about the safety of those in your care. If you seem to be more interested

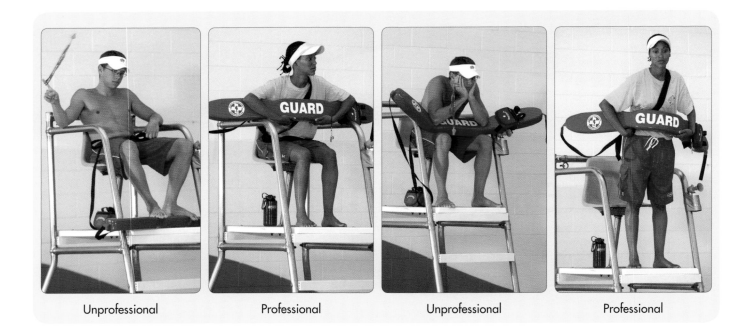

| Unprofessional | Professional | Unprofessional | Professional |

in goofing around with your coworkers or kids at the pool than being professional, this image will not only affect the opinion others have of you, but of the facility you represent. Your actions speak louder than your words. There are two kinds of behaviors you can project: those that enhance your image and those that demean your image.

Professional Behaviors

There are several things you can do every day to build up your professional image, including

- Wearing a clean, neat uniform that distinguishes you from the crowd
- Maintaining excellent posture. When sitting this includes having your feet flat, shoulders forward, rescue tube across your lap, with strap gathered
- Keeping focused and following StarGuard best practices
- Behaving as you expect others to behave
- Speaking to others as you wish to be spoken to

Unprofessional Behaviors

There are some behaviors that are not appropriate for lifeguards, which harm your professional image. Make a conscious effort to eliminate any of these behaviors while on the stand or in view of patrons:

- Slouching
- Whistle twirling
- Looking bored; looking at watch frequently
- Sitting with legs crossed or leaning your head on your hand(s)
- Socializing

- Talking on the phone
- Reading, smoking, gum chewing, or eating
- Belittling talk, gossiping, or using profanity
- Participating in pranks or encouraging unsafe patron behavior
- Appearing to be unfocused
- Using the rescue tube as a backrest or footrest
- Playing with rescue equipment
- Diving or cannonballing from the lifeguard stand

However, professionalism goes beyond your actions. It involves your commitment to performing at a high level. This commitment requires ongoing training, the ability to take responsibility for your performance, and good judgment.

Site-Specific Enrichment Training

Enrichment training, which is often referred to as in-service training, will be an important part of your professional development. Depending on the requirements of your facility, you can expect to spend several hours per month in enrichment training sessions. Topics should be geared toward maintaining your rescue and basic life support skills, use of the rescue equipment at your facility, physical conditioning, surveillance skills, and other information related to your responsibilities. Enrichment (in-service) training conducted where you work enhances your development in the following ways:

- Validating that you can perform and helping you gain confidence (this will be evident not only to your employer, but also to yourself)
- Allowing you to practice skills on the equipment available at your facility, while following the facility Emergency Action Plan (EAP)
- Developing teamwork with your coworkers
- Identifying areas of concern and developing more effective EAPs
- Building endurance and stamina, especially with physical conditioning
- Reinforcing your knowledge of workplace safety standards

Accountability

Expect to be involved in some evaluation system such as a lifeguard audit or review that measures your ability to perform your prevention, surveillance, aquatic rescue, emergency care, and professional skills. Whether your supervisors or an outside agency conduct this evaluation, it will provide you with an accurate picture of how well you focus on the important objectives of your job.

The first part of a lifeguard review, which is usually conducted without your knowledge that you are being watched, documents your level of professionalism, the prevention strategies you are using, and the level of surveillance you are providing. The second part usually consists of an aquatic rescue and emergency care scenario to evaluate your ability to manage an emergency situation. The objectives of an audit or review are as follows:

- Document your ability
- Identify any areas that need improvement so remediation can be conducted
- Recognize and award you for outstanding performance

Decision-Making Skills

As a lifeguard you will often need to make quick decisions. Your ability to use sound judgment to make decisions may mean the difference between saving a life or not. What types of decisions might you have to make? What would you decide if the following thoughts were going through your head?

- "I wonder if that is a shadow on the bottom or if I'm just seeing things. Should I go check it out or wait to see if it moves or goes away?"
- "The water is a bit cloudy and I can't see the bottom. Should I close the pool even though I know people will be upset?"
- "Should I put on sunscreen or get a tan?"
- "My replacement didn't show up on time, and I have to be somewhere. Should I leave?"
- "My friends want me to go with them to a baseball game. Should I call in sick even though I know the pool will be short a lifeguard?"

These are just a few of the types of decisions that you will make every day. Depending on the choice you make, they could have devastating long-term consequences. Your decisions should be based on the principles that value life, including yours, above all else. The decisions you make outside of the workplace can also have serious consequences. You might think that what you do on your own time doesn't matter, but the effects of substances such as alcohol or drugs can carry over into your working hours, even though the actual activity happened the night before.

One of the serious consequences of using poor judgment could be that your actions contribute to the injury or death of a patron at your facility. If this occurs, you could be held legally liable and found negligent.

Legal Liability

The legal system in the United States allows a lawsuit to be filed any time there is a perceived wrong. Filing a lawsuit puts into motion a series of events to determine the details of the alleged wrongdoing. The person filing the lawsuit, called the plaintiff, must prove that the other person, called the defendant, caused the injury either through action or inaction and that the injury could have been anticipated and therefore could have been prevented.

Only a judge or jury can decide whether the people named in the lawsuit were guilty of negligence. Before going to trial, a judge may determine that there is not enough evidence of wrongdoing or refuse to hear the case, or the parties involved may settle the case. In any event, simply naming someone in a lawsuit does not mean that they are guilty; they must be found to be so in a court of law.

The legal process is time consuming, emotionally draining, and expensive. If an injury or drowning event happens while you are lifeguarding and a lawsuit were filed, it would likely name your employer, you, and possibly others as defendants. In most instances, your employer would cover the legal costs to defend you. In some states, if you work for a municipality or governmental agency, you cannot be held liable.

However, if you are working as an independent contractor or for someone other than your primary employer (such as for an after-hours party for which the host is paying you directly), you can be held liable. It is important for you to understand the different types of employment status and the possible consequences in the event of legal action. If you are unsure of your status, be sure to ask, and consider legal advice.

To be considered an employee, you are required to fill out government withholding tax forms. Legitimate employers follow state and federal labor laws as well as occupational safety regulations, pay employment tax, as well as provide worker's compensation insurance in case you are injured on the job. All of these provisions are designed for your protection. If you are asked to work without filling out employment tax forms, the person hiring you may be considering you as an independent contractor and you will likely not be covered by worker's compensation or liability insurance should you get injured, or should a lawsuit be filed against you. In this instance, you should consider purchasing liability insurance. Be sure you understand your employee status and the possible consequences before accepting any lifeguarding job.

Lifeguarding in Difficult Situations

You might imagine that lifeguarding in a crowded, high-intensity environment would be a difficult situation. It could be, but that situation has a built-in excitement level that will help keep your vigilance high. A high-intensity environment

is also likely to have a large staff and a risk management system in place. These support systems actually serve to make the situation less difficult for you.

It is much more difficult to lifeguard in a quiet, low-intensity environment such as a one-guard facility or a pool where "nothing ever happens." Maintaining a high level of vigilance and professional behavior competes with complacency. You must keep the "fear factor" of the possibility of an emergency foremost in your mind at all times in order to consistently execute best practices in a low-stress environment.

Another difficult environment is if you are asked to lifeguard outside of your workplace such as for special events or parties at private homes. Often in these situations the host does not expect you to enforce rules because they don't want to spoil the fun and they do not understand the risks. Rescue equipment may not be available, and you may not be familiar with emergency procedures for that location. Unless you are representing, and being paid by, your employer in after-hours situations, you will not be covered by liability insurance unless you have your own policy. In these situations, make sure the host clearly defines what is expected of you, and get these expectations and a release from liability in writing.

Lifeguarding for Special Populations

Most people know someone with a disability or may even have one themselves. A disability occurs when a health condition or disorder results in an inability to perform typical functions, such as walking, learning, working, eating, grooming, and enjoying recreation. A disability can be caused by conditions at birth, genetic reasons, trauma, or illness later in life.

Some people who come to your facility may have disabling conditions that cause them to function differently. These people might visit an aquatic facility alone or accompanied by family members or a caregiver. As medical science continues to advance, you can expect more and more people with disabilities to live and remain in the community. Your professional responsibility should be to help people with disabilities enjoy the aquatic recreational environment with dignity. Because a person with a disability may function differently than a person without a disability, you may have to communicate with him or her in a different manner and consider additional safety issues.

Communication

Do not make assumptions about the abilities of a person with a disability. When you talk with a person with a disability, the following guidelines will help you communicate effectively:

- Use person-first language, such as "person with a disability" instead of "disabled person."
- Don't raise your voice; speak in a normal tone.
- When providing assistance to people with disabilities, first ask if they want help, and if so, ask how they would like to be helped. Ask the person directly rather than speaking to the caregiver about the person.
- Make certain that assistive features of the facility, such as pool lifts, are clean and in working order.
- Talk to the patron the same way you would want someone else to talk to a member of your family, or how you would want to be talked to.

Safety

When enforcing safety regulations, keep in mind that these rules are meant to keep all patrons safe, including people with disabilities. However, you can be flexible about rules for a patron with a disability as long as being flexible doesn't create a safety hazard. To keep all pool patrons safe, follow these guidelines:

- When a person with a disability enters the pool, note whether he or she is alone or accompanied by a family member or caregiver.
- If a patron with a disability breaks a pool rule, warn him or her and explain the rule.
- Watch a person with a disability when he or she is in the water. Some of the person's normal movements may look like distress, but are not. Watch for *changes* in the disabled person's movement patterns. If you notice something different or unusual, target the person, assess the situation, and decide whether you need to take action.
- Some people with disabilities will be accompanied by assistive animals, such as dogs, cats, or even monkeys. These are well-trained assistants that are allowed on the pool deck but not in the water in most circumstances.

What to Expect From Your Employer

The StarGuard course provides the information you need to understand the objectives of lifeguarding, teaches you the required physical skills, and suggests best practices as methods to help you perform. However, each aquatic facility is different, with different types of rescue equipment and procedures. Therefore, it is your responsibility to make sure that your employer provides you the necessary equipment and supplemental training and support to do your job. At a minimum, your employer should provide the following:

- Personal protection equipment, such as gloves and barrier mask
- Rescue tube
- Umbrella or shade
- Drinking water
- Lifeguard identification, such as a uniform
- Communication or signal device
- Telephone with EMS (9-1-1) access
- First aid supplies
- A break from scanning at least every hour
- Ability to change position so that you can stay alert and can scan the bottom
- Orientation to and practice of the facility emergency action plan
- Training in how to handle hazardous materials and in chemical safety if you are responsible for pool maintenance
- Orientation to and practice with the rescue equipment, such as backboard, automated external defibrillator, and oxygen
- Orientation to facility operating procedures
- Ongoing enrichment training
- Ongoing performance assessment
- Coverage under a liability insurance policy or immunity from liability

If your employer does not provide this support, you may be in a position in which it is impossible for you to perform at minimum standards.

What Your Employer Will Expect From You

A big part of being professional is being a good employee. This may be your first job and you are just entering the workforce. It is important to know what will be expected so that you don't make mistakes that could jeopardize your job, or ruin opportunities in the future. Just as you need support from your employer to do your job, your employer needs support from you to operate a safe facility. Your employer should require you to do the following:

- Provide proof of certification or authorization for lifeguard, CPR, first aid, and other required emergency care courses.
- Provide proof, through skills assessment, that you can perform rescue skills, including testing to see if you can descend to the deepest area of the pool to which you will be assigned.
- Uphold employment agreements, whether written or verbal. If you are hired with the understanding that you will work certain dates such as through the summer, it is very important that you honor this agreement.
- Find approved substitutes if you cannot work an assigned shift or follow the procedure set up at your facility. Calling in at the last minute or not showing up for a shift compromises the safety of everyone at the facility.

- Participate in a drug-testing program. Depending upon the regulations of your state, this program may include pre-employment screening, random testing, or post-incident testing.
- Exhibit a high level of professionalism and follow StarGuard Best Practices.

StarGuard Performance Goal

Project a positive image, have a commitment to improvement and accountability, and develop the ability to communicate and make responsible decisions.

StarGuard Best Practices

- Speak to patrons as you wish to be spoken to.
- Eliminate any behaviors that harm your professional image.
- Include behaviors that build up your professional image.
- Help people with disabilities enjoy aquatic recreation with dignity.
- Expect support from your employer.
- Fulfill the expectations of your employer.

Site-Specific Considerations

Objectives

Knowledge	Skill	Execution
After reading part VI, you should understand the following:	After instructor-observed practice and scenario training, you should be able to demonstrate the following:	After site-specific training, you should be able to do the following:
Waterpark The risk factors associated with play features, including slides, wave pools, winding river currents, free-form water areas, and children's play structures and strategies for minimizing or managing the risk The methods for enforcing rules on play features The methods for scanning wave pools, winding rivers, play structures, slide catch pools, and run-outs The general duties for lifeguards in a dispatch pool, a catch pool, a winding river, a wave pool, and a children's play area The importance of the E-stop to shut down water flow or wave action The considerations for emergency care on slides and in winding river currents and wave pools The importance of maintaining a professional image before large numbers of patrons	*Waterpark* Water rescue of a conscious person in moving water venues (e.g., wave action, current, catch pool) Water rescue of an unconscious person in moving water venues (e.g., wave action, current, catch pool) Water rescue of a person with a suspected spinal injury from moving water (e.g., wave pool, current, slide trough, zero depth area)	*Waterpark* Adapt prevention, surveillance, emergency care, aquatic rescue, professionalism, and personal safety skills to the needs of the waterpark environment

(continued)

(continued)

Knowledge	Skill	Execution
Waterfront and wilderness	*Waterfront and wilderness*	*Waterfront and wilderness*
The characteristics that distinguish types of waterfronts	Beach run-in entry	Adapt prevention, surveillance, emergency care, aquatic rescue, professionalism, and personal safety skills to the needs of the waterfront or wilderness environment
The risk factors in a waterfront or wilderness environment and strategies for minimizing or managing the risk	Modified belly-flop entry	Conduct a missing-person bottom search
The basic components of a site inspection	Donning and use of mask, fins, and snorkel	
The types of water activities that take place in remote wilderness settings	Approach stroke trailing rescue tube	
The factors to consider when screening a site for water activity	One-rescuer assist	
The factors to consider when conducting a skills screening to assess swimming ability	Seat carry	
The factors to consider when using rock slides	Cradle carry	
The components of a safety briefing for participants	Two-person extremity carry	
The general guidelines for crossing streams	Beach drag	
The importance of maintaining a constant count of patrons when scanning turbid water	Dragnet search, grid system search, swimming search line, and walking search line	
The methods for implementing a buddy system	Water rescue of a conscious person from a waterfront or wilderness venue	
The considerations when using rescue watercraft	Water rescue of an unconscious person from a waterfront or wilderness venue	
The common communication equipment and signals used in waterfront or wilderness settings	Water rescue of a person with a suspected spinal injury from a waterfront or wilderness venue	
The advantages of using a mask or goggles, fins, and snorkel for search and rescue in turbid water	HELP position	
The difference between search and rescue and search and recover	Huddle position	
The technique of sighting to mark the location of a drowning victim	Use of hand and whistle signals	
The concept of reach, throw, row, and go to prioritize rescue methods		
The usefulness of items that can be used as improvised rescue equipment		
The appropriate method to lift and remove a victim from the water when a backboard is not available		
Planning for long response times from EMS		
The appropriate methods for extricating an injured or unconscious person at the shoreline		
The benefits of the HELP and huddle positions to maintain body heat		

14

Lifeguarding at Waterparks and Play Features

If you will work at a waterpark or a facility with play features such as slides or moving water, you must complete the waterpark training module in addition to the basic StarGuard course. The waterpark module may be taught at the same time as your StarGuard course or presented as a separate training session.

Each section of this chapter covers a Starfish Risk Management Model component as it applies to lifeguarding in waterparks. These components are as follows:

- Prevention strategy
- Surveillance
- Emergency care and aquatic rescue
- Professionalism and personal safety

The unique features at waterparks or at aquatic facilities with attractions like those at a waterpark require additional prevention strategies.

Prevention Strategy

The most effective way to reduce the risk of injury to patrons enjoying waterpark attractions is to consistently enforce the rules for proper usage and regularly inspect the attractions. Each area or attraction should have safety and use instructions

Note: The material presented in this chapter supplements the main text.

clearly posted for patrons. These instructions should answer the following questions for each attraction:

- Must patrons be a maximum or minimum height before using this attraction?
- Must patrons be a maximum or minimum weight before using the attraction?
- Are certain types of apparel prohibited?
- Must patrons use a certain body position with this attraction? Are certain body positions prohibited?
- Is there a time or distance requirement between users?
- Is equipment such as tubes or mats required for use of this attraction? Is equipment prohibited from use on this attraction?

The attraction manufacturer usually provides guidelines for use that answer these questions, and then specific facility rules support these guidelines. It is important that you know the restrictions and rules for each area or attraction that you lifeguard and enforce these rules with all patrons.

The facility where you work should have checklist forms for you to use if you are responsible for inspecting a water attraction. Inspections are usually conducted each morning before opening. Even if you know that the attraction has been inspected, stay alert for problems that may develop during the day. Look for and report to your supervisor any of the following:

- Cracks
- Loose bolts
- Missing or broken pieces
- Nonfunctioning parts
- Unusual noises
- Increased frequency of injury or patron complaints
- Anything different or unusual

Besides knowing the rules for using waterpark attractions and inspecting them, you must also adjust your surveillance techniques when guarding in a waterpark.

Surveillance

Waterparks and facilities with many play features tend to attract a more transient crowd than a typical neighborhood pool; many patrons will be first-time visitors. You may go through your whole shift without recognizing any of the patrons in your care. As a result, you won't know the abilities of those who enter your zone, so treat all patrons as potential nonswimmers when you scan.

The specific features of a water attraction may affect your scanning pattern or posture. For example, the waterfalls and sprays of a children's play area may block your view from a stationary chair and make it necessary for you to walk or stand within the zone to scan. A sitting position at a wave pool may be adequate when the waves are off, but when the waves begin, a standing position may offer you a better view of the zone. The curves of a river-current attraction may make it necessary for you to walk the zone in order to cover all areas. Let's look at four common kinds of water attractions and how you should plan to guard them: slides, river-current features, wave pools, and other types of features.

Slides

The length of time it takes patrons to ride down the slide and then move out of the slide path determines dispatch (controlling and timing riders). Usually, a lifeguard or attendant at the top of the slide who can see the lifeguard monitoring the catch or run-out area controls when riders start down the slide. If you are in charge of dispatch, your responsibilities may include the following:

- Monitoring riders for height, size, age, ability, or other rider criteria that the slide manufacturer or your facility has set (Height sticks, signs marked with the minimum requirement, and prescreening guests and identifying eligible riders with wrist bands help with this task.)
- Instructing riders in proper body position for the slide
- Helping riders get into position on tubes or mats
- Issuing "go" commands when it is safe to dispatch
- Controlling the emergency stop (E-stop) to shut off water flow during an emergency
- Monitoring severe weather conditions
- Clearing patrons from the slide tower in the event of severe weather or other emergencies
- Communicating, via hand or flag signals, with the catch pool lifeguard

Your responsibilities in a slide catch pool, run out, or splashdown area may include the following:

- Helping patrons regain balance or stand up after landing
- Scanning for distress or drowning symptoms
- Helping patrons manage tubes as they make their way to the exit
- Directing patrons out of the slide path

- Enforcing rules and reminding patrons of ride procedures
- Keeping nonriders out of the splashdown or catch area
- Communicating, via hand or flag signals, with the dispatch lifeguard or attendant

River-Current Attractions

The presence of tubes in a river-current attraction may limit your ability to see under the surface of the water. Pay particular attention to the entry and exit areas of the river where tubes may get jammed and could possibly trap small children underneath. Keep these areas free of tubes. Your responsibilities at a river-current attraction may include the following:

- Directing patrons to enter and exit at designated points along the river (Multiple or controlled entry and exit areas minimize patron and tube congestion.)
- Helping patrons get in or out of tubes
- Enforcing rules and reminding patrons of ride procedures
- Pulling out unused tubes

Wave Pools

Wave pools provide various types of waves depending on the equipment used. Some wave machines create a surface back-and-forth water movement; others create a series of realistic, cresting waves that patrons can surf. Your facility orientation should include a description of the types of waves your machinery generates, the water depth in the wave pool during waves and during calm, the timing of wave sequences, and the locations and use of the E-stop buttons that shut down the wave action.

Facilities often use wave alarms, such as a siren or bell, to signal that wave action is about to begin. When an alarm sounds, be prepared for a sudden shift in patron use. Many guests will quickly leave the wave pool and others will rush to it in anticipation of the waves. Your wave pool responsibilities may include the following:

- Scanning for distress or drowning symptoms

- Monitoring the entrance and exit to the wave pool and restricting entrance and exit at the beach area only, not from the sides
- Monitoring and restricting use around or near wave chamber outlets or intakes
- Enforcing rules

Other Attractions

Inflatable slides, cable drops, rope challenges, climbing walls, and children's play structures are some of the common attractions found in aquatic facilities. Each of these attractions comes with manufacturer's guidelines for use. Your facility may add its own specific rules or procedures. Learn the rules and prevention strategies for all of the attraction areas at the facility where you lifeguard. Your main priority will always be to scan for distress or drowning symptoms.

Now that you know how to guard and what to watch for in a waterpark, let's discuss how to provide emergency care and aquatic rescue in a waterpark setting.

Emergency Care and Aquatic Rescue

The currents, waves, noise, and crowded conditions at aquatic attractions can all affect a water rescue. This is why you must practice rescue scenarios in a variety of conditions at the facility where you work. The more familiar you are with the conditions, the easier it will be for you to adapt your emergency care and rescue skills to meet the objective of the rescue.

If your facility protocol calls for backboarding patrons with a suspected spinal injury, practice this skill at each attraction. It may be necessary to backboard or provide other emergency care in a slide run out, at the top of a slide, in a moving

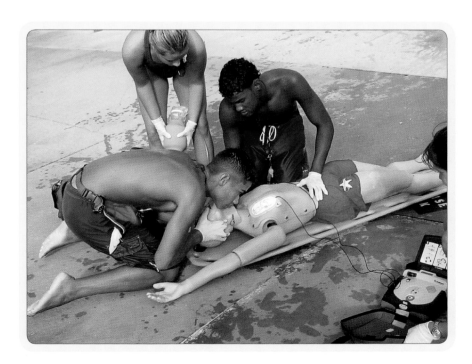

current, or in another situation. Using the objectives of spinal injury management as your foundation, adapt the backboarding procedures to the conditions at the attraction.

You also must be aware of the location and use of emergency stop buttons that will quickly shut off water flow or wave action. Your facility's emergency action plans detail how and when to activate the E-stop. The following are lists of emergency care and aquatic rescue strategies for slides, river-current attractions, and wave pools.

Slides

- Signal the dispatch guard or attendant to push the E-stop to prevent other patrons from sliding into your rescue scene.
- Keep hold of the rescue tube and remember to keep it between you and the other person at all times; it is likely that you will lose your balance and footing if you are in the path of the slide runoff.
- Spinal injury or sudden illness can occur inside the slide trough as well as on or at the base of the slide tower; practice rescue scenarios in these locations.
- Practice performing scenarios with unconscious victims in the catch pool and run-out area as well as at the top of the tower.

River-Current Attractions

- The pull of the current may complicate a rescue in a river-current attraction. Enter the water upstream of the distressed swimmer or drowning victim, and let the current move you to the person; if you jump in downstream, you will have to fight your way back against the current.
- The water depth in river attractions is usually shallow; always enter feetfirst with an ease-in entry or compact jump from the side.
- When you make contact with the person, don't try to fight the current, but rather move with the water flow to a takeout point.
- For a suspected spinal injury or to perform rescue breathing in the water, hit the E-stop to turn off the water flow and position yourself with your back to the current and the injured person so that the water is flowing from head to toe to help support his or her body.
- If the current is too strong, stop trying to stand on the bottom and float with the person while performing rescue breathing.
- If possible, your backup team should be prepared to follow you to an appropriate takeout point, rather than making you fight the current to get to a designated spot.

Wave Pools

- Push the E-stop button as part of your alert response and point toward the intended location of your rescue.
- Because the wave action movement of the water may not stop right away, time your compact jump so that you enter the water at the height of the wave where the water is deepest rather than at the trough where the water may be shallow.
- Be prepared to swim around and through a crowd of swimmers and tubes.

- Be prepared for longer extrication times in a wave pool because of the large size of the area, crowded conditions, wave action, and other factors; be ready to begin rescue breathing in the water if the drowning victim is unconscious.

- When placing the ventilation mask on the drowning victim, make a good seal to prevent the wave action from pushing water into the victim's nose and mouth.

- Because the wave action may not stop right away, practice rescues with the waves on to become comfortable with the movement and the effort required to perform rescue breathing in the waves.

- Practice extrication methods that are practical for the zero-depth beachfront area, such as those described in chapter 15.

Now let's consider what you need to do to act professionally and stay safe when guarding at a waterpark.

Professionalism and Personal Safety

The crowds that attend waterparks spotlight your need to present a professional image and serve as a role model to the guests in your care. Set a good example whenever you enjoy the water attractions at your facility. If you use the attractions, either during or outside of operating hours, follow the rules and regulations as though you were a patron.

In some ways, lifeguarding at a facility with play features or waterpark attractions is easier than lifeguarding a traditional pool. It's easier to maintain a high level of anticipation and vigilance when there is a lot of action. In other ways, lifeguarding

at a waterpark is more difficult. There are many more distractions in a waterpark environment. The noise of the crowd, the noise created by the slides or waves, and the activity level can all entice you to watch the fun rather than your zone. Be prepared to deal with and tune out these distractions.

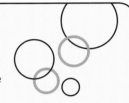

StarGuard Performance Goal

Adapt the prevention, surveillance, emergency care, aquatic rescue, and professionalism performance goals described in this text to the site-specific needs of a waterpark or facility with play features.

StarGuard Best Practices

- Enforce rules specific to each attraction.
- Notify your supervisor if you identify attraction hazards.
- Practice your emergency action plan at each attraction.
- Modify your scanning strategy and communication signals for the needs of the attraction.
- Know the location of the E-stop device to shut down water flow or wave action.

Lifeguarding at Waterfront and Wilderness Settings

A *restricted waterfront,* for purposes of the Star-Guard lifeguard training program, is a swimming area enclosed by lines, docks, or piers within an open body of water and the accompanying beach. The specialty training in this waterfront module helps you understand and manage the unique challenges of a restricted waterfront environment.

If you will work at a restricted waterfront, you must complete the waterfront training module in addition to the basic StarGuard course. The waterfront module may be taught at the same time as your StarGuard course or be presented as a separate training session.

Note: The material presented in this chapter supplements the main text.

Lifeguards who work at a *nonrestricted waterfront,* such as ocean beach with no enclosed swim area, must have additional open-water and surf rescue skills that are outside the scope of the StarGuard training program. Open-water or surf rescue training for beach lifeguards usually is conducted by the agency responsible for providing protection at the beach and should follow the guidelines of organizations such as the United States Lifesaving Association (USLA). Many agencies that operate surf beaches use StarGuard training as a prerequisite and then provide additional USLA accredited or other surf rescue training as the operating standard of care. If you work at a nonrestricted waterfront you must obtain this site-specific training from your employer.

A wilderness waterfront is defined by the following criteria:

- Travel time of more than an hour to the nearest hospital
- Existence of uncontrollable or hazardous environmental conditions such as weather, temperatures, moving and turbulent water, and rocks and other submerged hazards
- Existence of uncontrollable or hazardous terrain, such as narrow trails, swamps, or wide bodies of water, for evacuation
- Equipment limitations that may require improvisation, specialized equipment, or techniques

Wilderness StarGuard is an excellent training opportunity for people whose job might require them to manage or assist in aquatic emergencies in remote environments. These occupations include camp counselor, wilderness backpack leader, canoe expedition leader, park ranger, scout leader, adventure race coordinator, sailing instructor, and private expedition group leader.

The wilderness module may be taught at the same time as your StarGuard course or provided as an add-on module for lifeguards currently authorized by StarGuard or certified through a nationally recognized lifeguard training agency. *The materials presented here are a supplement to the main text.*

Each section of this chapter covers a Starfish Risk Management Model component as it applies to lifeguarding at waterfronts or in wilderness settings. These components are as follows:

- Prevention strategy
- Surveillance
- Emergency care and aquatic rescue
- Professionalism and personal safety

Let's begin by looking at prevention strategies such as site inspections and at specific strategies just for wilderness settings.

Prevention Strategy

Waterfront and wilderness areas present unique risks that you must manage in order to provide a safe environment for swimmers. Some ways to manage risks are inspecting sites frequently and, in wilderness settings, choosing appropriate sites for aquatic activities. Other prevention strategies include preparing participants for aquatic activities, following precautions for stream crossings, and following precautions during severe weather, especially when lightning is present.

Site Inspections

Because hazards at outdoor water areas often change over time, you must check waterfronts and wilderness water areas for hazards frequently. Depending on your location, your responsibilities for a site inspection may include the following:

- Clear the beach or swim area of debris, such as glass, cans, branches, hooks, food and drink containers, and human or animal waste.
- Check that appropriate rescue equipment is available, which for protected waterfronts may include rescue watercraft, mask, fins, snorkel, scuba gear, binoculars.
- Place equipment in a rescue-ready position. Determine the best rescue-ready position by conducting rescue scenarios. After each scenario evaluate how long it took the rescue equipment to reach the scene and how practical it is to keep equipment in various locations.
- Check that appropriate communication equipment is available, which for protected waterfronts may include two-way radios, bullhorn, public address system, flags, cell phones (if service is available), or other means to communicate with patrons across open spaces.

Wilderness Aquatic Activities

Aquatic activities and access to remote places have changed radically over the past 10 years. We used to visualize a trip to a rectangular neighborhood swimming pool or the waterfront at a camp just outside of town when we thought of group swimming. Today, many organized groups visit remote places and find themselves swimming in rivers or creeks, springs, lakes, or the ocean while participating in activities such as the following:

- Paddling in flat water or moving water
- Sailing
- Backpacking
- Mountaineering
- Canyoneering
- Day hiking to swim holes
- Team building challenge courses
- Adventure racing
- Snorkeling
- Survival training
- Military training

Organizations offering these activities include the following:

- Paddling schools
- Wilderness-based youth programs and camps
- Backcountry guide services
- University outing programs
- Clubs and organized public outing groups

- Make sure you can receive cell phone and radio signals before you need them in an emergency. Keep in mind that when dialing 9-1-1 from a cell phone, you may reach an emergency dispatch service from a county different than you had expected.
- Monitor the environment. Post or announce weather and water conditions along with warnings about restricted areas.
- Swim and walk the area to identify holes, drop-offs, rocks, or other hazards.
- Identify currents.
- Identify underwater obstructions.
- Check the water level and depth.

If you are inspecting a waterfront, you must also complete the following tasks:

- Check the depth under floating docks; the water depth at lakes linked to dam systems can change significantly from day to day.

- Check docks and piers for unsafe conditions.
- Make sure that the buoys, ropes, or docks marking the swim area are secure and that the transition safety zone between swimmers and boats is clearly identified.
- Test the water at restricted waterfronts for contaminants and bacteria; these may be caused by waterfowl or storm runoff. Health department regulations determine how often you test.
- Make sure that required safety equipment is located in the rescue watercraft and that the watercraft meets Coast Guard regulations.
- Make sure rescue equipment is available at all surveillance sites.
- Notify the appropriate authority, such as rangers or headquarters, that you have completed your safety checks and are ready to open.

If you are inspecting a wilderness setting, also do the following:

- Look for areas of questionable water quality, based on color, water flow, and an obvious source of contamination such as waterfowl feces or runoff.
- Assess the temperature of the water so that you can determine how long people should stay in the water. The colder the water, the shorter the swim times you should allow.
- Look for other site users, such as boaters, swimmers, fishermen, and determine their needs. If necessary, modify your activity to share the program site with other users.
- Look for signs of animal traffic and dwelling areas for wildlife such as snakes, beavers, frogs, and fish. If necessary, modify your activity to avoid wildlife dwellings and avoid animal traffic areas.

Strategies for Wilderness Settings

In addition to the site inspection outlined in the previous section, lifeguards in a wilderness setting must take additional precautions to secure participants' safety. The following steps are part of a comprehensive safety strategy for aquatic activities in the wilderness.

- Site screening. Before allowing participants to enter the water, inspect each wilderness water site to determine if it is appropriate and safe for use. This inspection often requires in-water evaluation. A person who has completed the Wilderness StarGuard training course must directly supervise any other person who is in the water inspecting an aquatic recreation site for recreational swimming. Use the following criteria to help determine if a wilderness site is suitable for swimming:
    - Access to the site is free of hazards or hazards can be minimized.
    - The swimming area is free of underwater hazards.
    - If you will allow participants to jump off rocks or ledges, the water must be deeper than 12 feet (3.7 meters) and the height of the jump must be less than 12 feet.
    - If the area contains rock slides, a slide can be no steeper than an estimated 30 degrees, and it must end in an area that is at least 3 feet deep (.9 meter) and free of obstructions.

If a site meets these criteria, look for appropriate entrances and exits to the water. Then identify swimmer and nonswimmer areas and determine appropriate boundaries for each. Finally, identify surveillance zones and decide how to provide surveillance.

- Safety briefings. Most insurance companies in the United States that service outdoor recreation businesses and organizations require that guides and trip leaders identify risks to the client before the activity starts. When clients have had the opportunity to evaluate the activity risk and willingly choose to participate, they have then assumed some responsibility for their actions. Many organizations identify "acknowledgement of risk" in both a written release form and a safety briefing. As a trip leader you are considered the expert, and it is your duty to warn. A safety briefing should include the following components:
  - Introduction. Communicate the fact that everyone shares the responsibility for safety.
  - Specifics. Communicate the inherent dangers, explain rules, demonstrate techniques, and explain emergency procedures.
  - Participant responsibility. Communicate the behavior you expect.
  - Close. Allow participants to ask questions and review key points. A sample safety talk outline is included in appendix C.

- Stream crossings. On a backpack trip you will often have to cross streams. Choose crossing sites that offer participants minimal challenge and risk. The following are general guidelines:
  - Cross streams with hip belts and sternum straps unfastened.
  - Walk across a log or series of rocks; stay low and plan for mishaps on slick terrain.
  - Cross streams where the current is weakest.
  - Cross streams where the water is less than knee deep for the shortest participant; consider not crossing if the moving water is higher than this.
  - Wear shoes or footwear that will protect your feet and toes as well as provide better traction on rocks.

- ○ When crossing in a swift current, feet should face upstream for better traction against the water flow and to avoid foot entrapment, which is the leading cause of death in moving water that is above knee depth.
- ○ Use walking sticks or trekking poles to provide additional points of contact.
- ○ Wade with a partner for stability. Face each other and push forward on the other person's shoulders.
- ○ Set up a hand line for group members, but never tie a rope to anyone!
- ○ In alpine areas, beware of snow bridges and other false debris bridges.

Lightning Safety in the Wilderness

In wilderness settings, seek shelter in a small stand of trees that are roughly the same height and diameter. Instruct group members to spread out approximately 50 feet (about 15 meters) from each other away from standing water and try to minimize contact with the ground. For example, squatting, with your feet together and hands off the ground, will reduce the ability of lightning to access your body. Group leaders should position themselves on either end of the group, not next to each other. When seeking shelter, avoid high places, open fields, beaches, isolated trees, trails, water line areas, areas of still water (ditches), or any place with metal objects.

Surveillance

In most waterfront and wilderness water settings you cannot scan the bottom, so it becomes even more important to keep nonswimmers in shallow water and to keep track of all swimmers. Setting up clear boundaries for safe swimming and nonswimming areas, screening people to assess their swimming skills, and conducting buddy checks and safety breaks will help you accomplish this. In waterfront settings, it may also be helpful for someone to provide surveillance from a watercraft.

To help keep people safe, mark safe swimming areas and nonswimmer areas in the following ways:

- In a restricted waterfront, clearly mark the areas with buoy lines or a combination of piers, docks, and lines. When possible, divide the water into areas for specific uses, such as swimming, diving, and sliding.
- In a wilderness setting, distinguish the safe swimming areas and nonswimmer areas by identifying trees, rocks, or other items that can mark the boundaries.
- Communicate to participants the clear boundaries between the swimming areas and nonswimmer areas.
- Restrict nonswimmers to water that is less than waist deep or require them to wear life jackets.

When you guard in a waterfront area, keep track of patrons by doing the following:

- Maintain a constant count of patrons in your zone with each scan or sweep.

- Visually follow the path of patrons swimming to or from floating platforms.
- Allow only one diver or slider to enter the water at a time. Allow subsequent divers or sliders to enter only after you have seen the preceding diver or slider return to the surface and move out of the entry area.
- In a wilderness setting, do not allow diving; require a feet-first entry.
- In cloudy water at waterfronts it may not be possible to perform a bottom scan, so visually group, categorize, or place swimmers in quadrants as you sweep your eyes across the zone.
- Continuously count people in the zone whenever practical.
- Mentally sort swimmers into groups according to ability, age, or risk factors during successive scans.
- Do not allow underwater swimming.

Screening Swimmers

When it is necessary to assign people to swimming or nonswimming areas, you must first assess their swimming abilities by screening them. You must also assess swimming ability during group outings to a water area before allowing people to participate in water activities in which they will not wear a personal flotation device (life jacket) and the water is more than waist deep. Don't rely on a swimmer's assessment of his or her own swimming ability before testing. The purpose of the skill screening is to identify participants who do not have the endurance or ability to comfortably keep their heads above water without a life jacket.

A skills test must reflect the skills needed for the activity and conditions. As an example of a general skills screening, consider asking participants to swim approximately 50 yards (or meters), tread water without using their hands for one minute. In a wilderness setting it may be appropriate to ask participants to tread water and stay afloat while tying and untying their shoes or removing and replacing clothing. Any or all of these activities, adjusted for the circumstances, will help you assess the participants' water skills. Your objective is to have each participant demonstrate to you in a measurable way his or her swimming ability appropriate for the activity. To conduct a skills screening in either a waterfront or a wilderness setting, follow these guidelines:

- Choose specific screening activities appropriate to your environment. Your test must reflect the skills needed for the activity and conditions.
- Choose a screening area in which the water is no more than waist deep for the participants.
- The screening area should be free of sudden drop-offs or submerged objects such as logs or other debris.
- Conduct screenings near the shoreline or along a dock.
- Participants should enter the water feetfirst and wear foot protection.
- Do not allow underwater swimming.

Based on the results of the screening, assign the person to either a swimming area or a nonswimming area. You might also require the nonswimmer to use a life jacket. Document the results of the swim tests. Include the date, time, swimmer's name, age, and skill assessment outcome.

When managing large groups, consider using some type of identification that shows which people belong in which areas. In restricted waterfront settings, one way to do this is to provide a wristband or break-away necklace band to each patron who has completed skills screening. Use one color to designate a swimmer and another to designate a nonswimmer.

Buddy System and Buddy Check

Another useful surveillance strategy is using a buddy system and calling for frequent safety breaks, during which all patrons get out of the water for a short time. In a buddy system, pair swimmers by ability. If the pair's ability is not equal, the less-skilled swimmer defines the swim area for that pair. Buddy swimmers must stay within sight of each other at all times. To identify which buddies are swimming and which have left the swim area, use one of the following methods:

- Keep a buddy board or swimmer chart on a note pad; buddy pairs must check in and check out with the specified staff person in charge of the chart.
- Designate two ball caps as "in" and "out"; swimmers place their names in the hat that designates their swimming status.
- Have each swimmer leave a similar article of clothing, such as a shirt or cap, in a designated area to indicate to staff which swimmers are in and out.

Besides using a buddy system, you may want to use a buddy check (also called a safety break) as well. Simply signal a check after a set amount of time, asking all participants to get out of the water. A buddy check takes less than one minute to implement and allows you to make sure all participants are present and accounted for. Preassigned buddies or small groups account for each other.

Guarding From a Rescue Watercraft

Guarding the area from a watercraft in the water is another way to keep track of swimmers at a waterfront. You can use watercraft at a waterfront to patrol the perimeter of a swim area or to serve as an anchored surveillance position. Watercraft can be human powered, such as a paddleboard, kayak, canoe, or rowboat, or motor powered, such as a jet ski, inflatable boat, or small motorboat. Your facility

should provide you with an orientation and instruction in safety practices for the specific watercraft you might use. You should also practice rescue scenarios using the watercraft.

For motor-powered watercraft, it is ideal to have two lifeguards on each craft: one serving as an operator and one providing surveillance. When this is not possible and the operator also provides surveillance, it is important to have a good communication device, such as an air horn or radio. Rescue watercraft should carry the following equipment:

- Life jackets for each occupant and at least one extra life jacket for a potential passenger
- Oars or paddles
- Lines (ropes)
- Flotation devices that can be thrown
- A rescue tube
- A bailer (except for a paddleboard)
- A waist pack or kit with ventilation mask, gloves, and first aid supplies
- Water or fluids for hydration
- Communication devices, such as whistle, air horn, radio, signal flags
- Depending on the size of the craft, the U.S. Coast Guard might require motor-powered craft to carry additional equipment such as an anchor and line and a fire extinguisher.

Emergency Care and Aquatic Rescue

Providing emergency care and aquatic rescue is more difficult at waterfronts and in wilderness settings than at pools because of natural barriers such as rocks, cliffs, vegetation, and shoreline. and the distance between the site and emergency help. However, by preparing for rescues, developing emergency action plans and methods for search and rescue (and search and recover), and determining safe ways to perform rescues, your organization should be ready to deal with these circumstances.

Preparation for Rescue Situations

Before an emergency situation arises, your organization should establish a communications system for lifeguards. At waterfronts, preparation should include training on how to use underwater search equipment such as a mask or goggles, fins, and snorkel.

Communications System for Lifeguards

Wilderness waterfronts and swimming areas surrounded by rocks can become noisy when used by small groups. You need some means besides yelling to communicate with participants and other lifeguards or rescuers. Systems include hand or whistle signals or a combination of the two and other signaling devices such as paddles, clothing or flags, air horns, and two-way radios and cell phones. You and the other lifeguards or rescuers must agree on what the signals mean before allowing participants to enter the water. Crossed or misunderstood signals lead to failed water rescue attempts and could mean the difference between success and catastrophe. Clear communication conserves time and energy at a rescue scene. The most commonly used communications in a wilderness setting are whistle blasts and hand signals.

Whistle Signals

- Two short blasts. "Give me your attention."
- A series of three or more blasts. "Danger, distress, activate the emergency action plan" or "Get out of the water! Assisting rescuers and staff, give me your attention."

Hand Signals

- Raised fist. "I need help. Come here."
- Multiple taps on the top of the head. "Are you O.K.?" and "I am O.K." Two taps on the top of the head. "Cover my zone."
- Crossing and uncrossing the arms above the head. "I am not O.K."
- Arms crossed above head in the form of an X. "Missing swimmer."

Mask or Goggles, Fins, and Snorkel

Wearing swim goggles or a mask will let you see better under the water when performing a rescue or conducting an underwater search. Here are some tips for using goggles or a mask:

- Be sure that the mask (or goggles) fits correctly, forming a watertight seal around your eyes to prevent leaking. Goggles can be used if you will be swimming underwater in shallow depths (under 10 ft or 3 m) and for short periods of time. If you will be deeper, the water pressure against goggles may become uncomfortable, and you should consider using a mask.

- To prevent fogging, wipe the interior surface with an antifog agent or a small amount of saliva.

- To remove water from a leaking mask, tilt your head back slightly. Press the top of the mask faceplate toward your face; the bottom of the mask will move slightly away from your face. Exhale strongly through your nose to push the water out of the mask.

- To prevent or relieve mask squeeze (an uncomfortable pressure against your face and eyes when you descend) exhale small bursts of air from your nose. This air will equalize the pressure in the mask to that of the pressure in the water.

- To prevent or relieve pressure in your ears when you descend, you must equalize your ears. Choose a method that works for you: blow gently against a pinched nose, pinch your nose and swallow, or pinch your nose and yawn.

Using a snorkel allows you to keep your face submerged as you search. Use a snorkel keeper to secure the snorkel to the head strap of your mask or goggles. Place the mouthpiece in your mouth and hold it in place lightly with your lips and teeth. Breathe slowly and deeply. When you are ready to submerge completely and swim deeper, take a relaxed deep breath and hold it, and pull yourself down under the water. Do not hyperventilate (caused by breathing rapidly several times, then holding your breath) before submerging.

When you surface, clear your snorkel by exhaling strongly with a short burst of air to force the water from the tube. Exhale to clear the tube only when you are sure that you are at the surface and the top of the snorkel is no longer submerged. When the water has been expelled, inhale through your mouth and continue relaxed breathing.

Wearing fins will increase your propulsion through the water. Fins come in two styles: full heel and open heel, which usually requires you to wear booties. Whenever possible, put on your fins when you are in the water or at the water's edge. If you have to walk with fins on, move sideways or backward to prevent tripping. When you swim, kick with slow, smooth kicks. The movement should come from your hips, and your knees should have a slight to moderate bend, depending on the style of fin.

While swimming with goggles or mask, snorkel, and fins, keep your arms either in front or in a relaxed position along your sides. If you are performing a bottom search, keep your hands forward and sweep them toward the sides to feel for the victim. To surface dive while wearing goggles or mask, snorkel, and fins, do the following:

1. Tuck your chin to your chest and press your head and shoulders forward.
2. Bend your hips to roll into a pike or tuck position.
3. Lift your legs to extend your body; this movement allows you to descend headfirst. Move your hands in front of your body into the search position, which will also protect you from submerged hazards.

Missing Persons Emergency Action Plan

In a waterfront or wilderness setting your organization should have a specific emergency action plan (EAP) in place in case someone is reported missing. Until the person is found, there is no way to know if he or she is on land or submerged under the water. **Because time is critical in rescuing a submerged victim, immediately begin a bottom search when looking for a missing person.** Customize the emergency action plan based on circumstances, and consider these factors:

- Number of staff available
- Number of bystanders usually available
- Response time of EMS or search and rescue/recover teams
- Water depth
- Water temperature
- Water clarity
- In-water hazards
- Search methods appropriate for the waterfront or wilderness setting
- Equipment or watercraft available

Regardless of the circumstances, a missing person EAP should include these elements:

- A specific communication signal to indicate a missing-person situation
- A designated staging area for all staff and bystanders
- Two groups of searchers: one water based and one land based; begin the water search immediately

Those searching on land should gather information about the person, including name, age, and description, and start the search in the immediate area, including the bathhouse, campsite, and parking lot. The search should then extend to the surrounding area, including woods, cabins, and outbuildings.

Search and Rescue or Search and Recover

Search and rescue refers to situations in which it is likely that a missing person will be found quickly enough that survival is possible. Search and recover refers to situations in which so much time has passed that survival is unlikely.

At a waterfront, enough lifeguards and other rescuers should be available that search and rescue is your initial protocol. Search the bottom of the swim area first because brain damage and death can occur within minutes of submersion; therefore, your window for performing search and rescue is relatively short. For this reason, it should take no more than five minutes to completely search the swim area. The specific conditions at your facility—including the number of staff, equipment, water depth, availability of bystanders, and search techniques—determine how large an area you can search within this time frame.

Search and rescue efforts should begin near the place where the person was last seen. If possible, visually mark the spot where the person was known to have submerged by "sighting," or lining up, the spot with a stationary object on the shore. Sighting from several positions and vantage points further helps pinpoint the area. If currents are present, begin the search downstream because it is likely that the person has been pushed to a different location by the moving water.

Search and rescue efforts by lifeguards and bystanders should continue until the person is found or until a search and recover dive team (usually EMS, fire, or police professionals) arrives. When EMS arrives, continue your search until whoever is directing the EMS effort directs you to stop or gives other instructions. Search strategies for restricted waterfront areas may include the following:

- Dragnet search. String a weighted net on a section of PVC or hold at each end. Begin the search near the person's last known location, and follow a predetermined pattern to quickly move the net across the bottom of the swimming area. You may walk or move the net while swimming as long as the net reaches the bottom.

- Grid system. Some waterfronts may have lines or markers anchored along the bottom to help when conducting an underwater search. The search team, wearing goggles or mask, snorkel, and fins (or scuba gear, if trained to use such equipment) lines up along each grid mark and moves forward along the designated path.

- Swimming search line. This search method is similar to the grid system, but without the benefit of physical markings on the bottom. In shallow water where the bottom can be clearly seen, the search team should swim in a line, shoulder to shoulder. In deeper water, the search team should combine short surface dives to look and feel for a victim on the bottom. Surface dive to the bottom, swim and sweep with the arms for 10 to 15 feet (3 to 4.5 meters), surface, back up approximately 3 to 5 feet (1 to 1.5 meters) and repeat the process.

- Walking search line. The search team forms a line, facing the direction in which the search will begin, and hooks elbows. The line of rescuers moves forward while rescuers sweep the area in front and to the side with the feet and legs.

For all search strategies, if contact with the missing person is made, the rescuer immediately stops and signals to initiate the emergency action plan.

Performing search and recovery in a wilderness setting may be more difficult than at a waterfront because of murky water and moving currents, which make a "point last seen" indistinguishable from the surrounding area. You and other rescuers must search the "point last seen" rapidly with quick dives. After these first few minutes have passed, the chances of a successful recovery and resuscitation decline significantly. However, drownings in cold water may be the exception to this case, so continue recovery attempts up to one hour or until the situation becomes unsafe for rescuers. When someone is reported missing in a wilderness setting, follow these steps:

- Activate the emergency action plan.
- Ask people on shore to help fix the point last seen.
- Pick out a landmark on an opposing shore in line with the point last seen to help identify the appropriate search area.
- Identify the time of submersion.
- Initially search the point last seen with either an in-water search by wading and swimming, a surface search by surface swimming or using a watercraft, or an underwater search with goggles or mask, fins, and snorkel.

Water Rescue

Now that you have found the person, you can begin the rescue. Rescues at a waterfront may require you to travel a long way to reach the person, and rescues in the wilderness require you to think about how best to execute the rescue, how to improvise rescue equipment, and how to stabilize a person with a spinal injury.

Rescues at a Waterfront

At a waterfront, you may need to swim a greater distance to make a rescue than in a pool. To save time, you may want to run down the shoreline to a position in line with the person and then enter the water. If the person is more than 10 yards (9 meters) from you, it may be faster to swim trailing the rescue tube rather than holding it. Stop about 10 feet (3 meters) from the person, pull your rescue tube into position and then complete the rescue.

Rescues in a Wilderness Setting

In a wilderness setting, a water rescue should be your last choice. The phrase "reach, throw, row, and go" identifies water rescue options in order of preference:

Reach. Extend a rope, flotation device, piece of clothing, pole, or branch to the person.

Throw. Throw a rope or a flotation device to the person.

Row. Paddle a canoe or row a boat to the person, and use the boat as a rescue platform.

Go. Swim out and perform an in-water rescue.

Throwing a buoy or rope can be effective, but often it is difficult for the person to find and maintain contact with a thrown object. When throwing an object, aim behind and upwind of the person (and upstream in moving water). Then pull the object toward the person. If you aim in front and fall short, you will waste valuable time pulling in the line and rethrowing. Be careful not to hit the person when you throw a flotation device to him or her.

If you must make a water rescue in a wilderness setting, you probably won't have equipment such as rescue tubes or backboards. However, you will usually have items that you can adapt for use as rescue equipment. These include the following:

- Walking sticks or trekking poles can be used as reaching devices.
- Rescue rope (floatable polypropylene, 30 feet long or 9 meters) can be thrown.
- Inflatable or noninflatable sleeping mattresses can be rolled to make a flotation device similar to a rescue tube.
- An inflatable rescue tube can be activated with a CO_2 cartridge when needed.
- A compressed sleeping bag can be put in a stuff sack to make a flotation device similar to a rescue tube.
- Water bottles can be emptied and placed in a stuff sack to create a flotation device.

When making a water rescue, you must decide how to enter the water based on your distance from the person and his or her condition. Use a compact jump when you are jumping from a height into water of any depth where there may be underwater obstructions. Use a protected water entry when entering from water level. The protected water entry is a modified belly flop, which will help you stay on the surface and protect your face and neck from possible injury. To perform this entry, do the following:

1. When you are about knee deep, push off with your legs and lean forward.
2. Arch your back and cross your arms in front of your face.
3. Your chest and abdomen should enter the water first. The more you are able to stay on the surface, the better you will be able to maintain a constant view of the person's position in the water.

Managing a spinal injury in a wilderness aquatic setting requires adaptation because you probably won't have a backboard, and the physical conditions could be challenging. Because someone with a spinal injury may be unable to maintain

appropriate body temperature, you must gently move the person to a dry, relatively flat spot where you can continue care. The objective remains the same as for a spinal injury that occurs in other conditions: to minimize movement of the head, neck, and spine. Follow these steps to manage a person with a suspected spinal injury:

1. Scan, target, assess, alert, and rescue using an improvised flotation device.
2. Perform in-water stabilization.
3. Move toward land with the support of a flotation device while monitoring the person's condition.
4. Once in shallow water, if there is a moving current, orient the person's body so that the head is upstream. This position will help minimize spine flexion.
5. Move the person to dry land using the Body Elevation and Movement (BEAM) method you learned in Wilderness First Aid training. Look at your surroundings and choose the shortest, least-obstructed route to your designated extrication point. You need a minimum of five rescuers to move the person no more than 50 feet (15.2 meters); a shorter distance is better. Place the lead rescuer at the head, with the others equally distributed to support the person's torso and hips. Just as in backboarding, the lead rescuer will guide the other rescuers' movements.

6. Extricate the person. The rescuer at the head leads the extrication. Lift and lower the person as one unit, keeping the person's ears in line with his or her shoulders and the shoulders in line with the hips at all times. Avoid moving the person's head toward his or her chest.
7. Splint the injured person's head and neck using an improvised head immobilization device (HID), then treat the person for shock. Items that can be rolled

and placed along the sides of the head (or along the sides and around the top of the head), then secured in place, can be used as an improvised HID. Such items might include a stuff sack, towel or blanket, ground pad, clothing, parka.

Managing an Unconscious Drowning Victim

Conditions specific to waterfront and wilderness areas may affect how you manage an unconscious drowning victim. You must be prepared for a potentially long response time for EMS and to extricate an unconscious drowning victim at a shoreline. The equipment you have available and the number of rescuers or bystanders you have to help will determine the techniques you use to get an unconscious drowning victim onto land to begin emergency care.

Waterfront areas are often in rural locations and may present a long emergency medical system response time. Plan your emergency procedures accordingly. For example, if your emergency oxygen equipment is capable of administering 15 minutes of oxygen and you can expect a 20-minute response, you should have an extra tank or two on site.

Wilderness settings also are likely to be far away from EMS help. Here are additional considerations to take into account when working in a wilderness setting:

- When advanced life support will be significantly delayed, consider terminating resuscitative efforts after 30 minutes if there are no signs of life.
- Continue CPR as long as possible for a victim who has drowned in cold water. Survival, even after long submersion times, is more likely if the water is cold.
- Continue CPR and rescue breathing as long as possible for people who have been struck by lightning.
- Collect a sample of the water from all drowning events that require resuscitation. The water may be needed to determine if contamination was present, which can be helpful for post-resuscitative care.
- Monitor drowning survivors closely because complications can occur after resuscitation, especially when a victim has been submerged in saltwater.
- Evacuate any person who has experienced a drowning event and has lost consciousness, has shortness of breath, is coughing up fluid or mucus, or has moving fluid sounds in the lungs.

Shoreline Extrication

Injured, ill, or unconscious people may need to be removed from the water or moved to another location away from the water's edge. Always lift with your legs, keeping your back straight and bending your knees. Keep your center of gravity low and the weight of the victim close to your body. Factors that may affect the type of extrication method you choose include the following:

- Size of waterfront obstructions, such as rocks and trees
- Size of the victim
- Whether or not you will use spinal-injury precautions
- Height from the water to the shore

- Equipment available
- Number of people available to assist

Extrication methods to use at waterfront or wilderness areas for people who are not suspected of having a spinal injury include the following:

- One-rescuer assist. Use this method if a person is conscious and can walk. Place the person's arm around your shoulders and your arm around his or her waist. Provide support and assistance as needed as you walk out. If a second rescuer is available, he or she should move to the other side of the injured person to provide additional support and assistance.

- Seat carry. This method requires two or three rescuers. Use it if a person is conscious but cannot walk. Two rescuers are at the person's upper body and place the person's arms around their shoulders. If there are only two rescuers and the injured person's size allows, rescuers can create a "seat" by joining hands under the person's upper legs and lifting. If a third rescuer is available, he or she can hold the person's legs and help carry the person out. You can perform the three-rescuer carry with the victim either faceup or facedown.

- Cradle carry. Use this extrication method for either a conscious or unconscious person, if you can pick up and carry the injured person. Hold the person just above the knees, and cradle your arm around the middle of his or her back.

• Two-person extremity carry. Two rescuers can use this extrication method on someone who is conscious or unconscious. One rescuer gets behind the person and prepares to lift by grasping under the person's arms. The second rescuer stands at the person's feet, between the legs, facing away from the person. This rescuer prepares to lift by grasping the person's ankles and pulling them into his or her body for support. For a larger person, back up and hold under the knees. Both rescuers lift the person at the same time and walk forward. The rescuer at the feet leads the way.

• Beach drag. One or more rescuers use this extrication method if a person is unconscious. When you get to shallow water, move behind the person and hold him or her under the armpits. Walk backward out of the water and up onto the beach. If the beach has a slope, position the victim with the head slightly downsloped to move blood flow away from the legs and toward the vital organs.

Professionalism and Personal Safety

Be aware of how the cold water often present in waterfront and wilderness areas can affect your endurance and swimming skills. Wear a wetsuit during training activities to prevent hypothermia, and maintain your physical conditioning through regular exercise. If you find yourself in the water and help is unlikely to arrive for a long time, you must conserve your energy and body heat. The heat escape lessening position (HELP) minimizes your exposure to the cold water. Follow these steps to get into the HELP position:

1. Draw your body into a ball as close as comfortable.
2. Minimize exposure of your body to the water and/or air. If possible, cover your head and neck with insulation such as clothing or headwear.
3. Work at staying mentally alert by reciting numbers, the alphabet, stories, and so on.
4. Minimize movement and focus on breathing slowly and easily.

If more than one person is in the water, you all can huddle by following these steps:

1. Get as close to others as possible, sharing and trapping body heat.
2. Keep tabs on how alert huddle members are. Encourage conversation or other activities such as singing or reciting to keep mentally alert. If a person is experiencing a diminished level of consciousness, tap him or her on the shoulder and shout words of encouragement. Have group members hold that person closer in order to conserve body heat.
3. Monitor group morale.

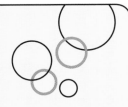

StarGuard Performance Goal

Adapt the prevention, surveillance, emergency care, aquatic rescue, and professionalism performance goals in this text to the site-specific needs of a waterfront or wilderness setting.

StarGuard Best Practices

- Frequently inspect swimming areas for hazards.
- If a person is missing, conduct a bottom search first.
- Plan and then practice search-and-rescue drills to determine the methods best suited to the physical conditions at your restricted waterfront.
- Maintain a constant count of patrons in turbid (cloudy) water conditions.
- Improvise rescue equipment and techniques in wilderness settings.

Appendix A

Sample First Aid Report

Date: _____ Time: _____ a.m. p.m.   Day: Sun Mon Tues Wed Thurs Fri Sat

Name of person: _____ Phone: _____

Street address: _____

City: _____ State: _____ ZIP: _____ Country: _____

Age: _____ Sex: M F   Parent/guardian name: _____

Under supervision of (at time of incident): _____ Relationship: _____

Location of incident: _____

Witnesses:

Name: _____ Phone: _____

Name: _____ Phone: _____

Nature of injury or illness (continue on back or attach narrative if necessary): _____

_____

Signs and symptoms (e.g., difficulty breathing, pain) _____

Allergies (Are you allergic to anything?) _____

Medical ID emblem (e.g., bracelet, necklace, tag) _____

Pain (Are you experiencing pain?) _____

Last oral intake (When did you last eat or drink?) _____

Events leading to injury (What were you doing when this happened?) _____

Onset (When did this start?) _____

Provocation (Has anything you've done made it worse?) _____

Quality (What kind of pain do you have? Sharp, dull, pressing, throbbing?) _____

Radiation (Is the pain in one place or does it spread?) _____

Severity (On a scale of 1 to 10, how severe is the pain?) _____

Time (How long have you felt this way?) _____

Was blood present? Yes No

Were gloves used? Yes No

(continued)

From *StarGuard: Best Practices for Lifeguards, Third Edition* by Jill E. White, 2006, Champaign, IL: Human Kinetics.

(continued)

Care provided: _____

_____

_____

Instructions given: _____

_____

_____

Person released to: Returned to facility   Parent/guardian   EMS   Other: _____

Was EMS notified?   Not necessary   Yes   Refused (see below)

If EMS was notified, was person transferred?   No   Yes, name of hospital: _____

Signature of rescuer or person completing this report: _____

Printed name of rescuer or person completing this report: _____

A person may refuse care if he or she meets all these criteria: (1) is older than 18; (2) is oriented to person (knows who he or she is), place, time, and situation; (3) exhibits no evidence of an altered level of consciousness or of alcohol or drug ingestion that impairs judgment; and (4) understands the risks and consequences of refusing care.

Refusal of Care and Acknowledgement of Information

I understand that the basic first aid care provided by the aquatic staff is not a substitute for care by EMS, a physician, or a hospital. I (or minor named above) have been offered one or more of the following services: EMS evaluation, medical care, and transportation; however, I am refusing the services offered. I have been advised and understand the risks and consequences of refusing advanced care and transport, including the fact that delay in treatment could be hazardous to my health and, under certain circumstances, could result in disability or death.

Release of Liability

By signing this form, I am releasing the attending lifeguards, the aquatic facility, and its agents of any liability or medical claims resulting from my decision to refuse the medical care and transport. I have read and understand the "Acknowledgement of Information" and "Release of Liability."

_____   Refused to sign
                Signature

Relationship (if for a child):   Parent   Guardian

From *StarGuard: Best Practices for Lifeguards, Third Edition* by Jill E. White, 2006, Champaign, IL: Human Kinetics.

Appendix B

Sample Rescue Report

Date: _____ Time: _____ a.m. p.m.   Day: Sun Mon Tues Wed Thurs Fri Sat

Name of person: _____ Phone: _____

Street address: _____

City: _____ State: _____ ZIP: _____ Country: _____

Age: _____ Sex: M F   Parent/guardian name: _____

Under supervision of (at time of incident): _____ Relationship: _____

Location of incident: _____

Witnesses (for unconscious or suspected spinal or severe injury):

Name: _____ Phone: _____

Name: _____ Phone: _____

Nature of rescue (attach narrative report if necessary):

_____ Distressed swimmer (mouth/nose/airway remained above water)

_____ Drowning (mouth/nose/airway was covered with water), but person remained conscious

_____ Unconscious person (contributing medical conditions unknown)

_____ Suspected spinal injury, in the water

_____ Suspected spinal injury, out of the water

Sex: Male   Female

Age: _____   (if unknown, approximate age)   0-4   5-9   10-18   19-35   36-60   60+

Medical ID emblem? (Bracelet, necklace, tag)   No   Yes, for: _____

Position: At edge or wall   On surface   Submerged below surface: 1-2 ft (0.3-0.6 m)   2-4 ft (.6-1.2 m)
        4-6 ft (1.2-1.8 m)   6-9 ft (1.8-2.7 m)   9-12 ft (2.7-3.7 m)   12+ ft (3.7+ m)

Location: Outdoors   Indoors

  Play structure   Wading pool   Diving well   Lap pool   Activity pool   Winding river
  Slide bottom   Spa   Wave pool   Waterfront   Other: _____

  Water depth: Less than 4 ft (1.2 m)   4-9 ft (1.2-2.7 m)   9+ ft (2.7+ m)

Events (rescue occurred during):   Recreational swim   Lap swim   Swim lessons   Swim team practice
  Swim meet   Dive team practice   Dive meet   Other: _____

Observation of distress or drowning: Oral yell   Facial expression   Struggling movement   Patron
notification   Lack of movement   View from underwater surveillance system   Other: _____

(continued)

From *StarGuard: Best Practices for Lifeguards, Third Edition* by Jill E. White, 2006, Champaign, IL: Human Kinetics.

(continued)

Provocation or possible contributing factors: Unsupervised child   Breath holding   Diving
   Exhaustion   Medical emergency   Horseplay   Intoxication or drugs   Rule infraction
   Nonswimmer   Peer pressure   Slipped off flotation device   Moved into water that was slightly too
   deep   Lost footing   Other: _____

Quality of water: Clear   Turbid   Other: _____

Race: Asian   Black   Hispanic   White   Other: _____

Supervision (child was supervised and accompanied by):   Parent/guardian   Group leader
   Relative/other adult   None

Temperature: Air: less than 70 °F (21 °C)   71-89 °F (21.6-31.6 °C)   over 90 °F (over 32 °C)
            Water: less than 70 °F (21 °C)   71-87° (21.6-30.5 °C)   over 88° (over 31.1 °C)

Was person injured? Yes   No   Was blood present? Yes   No

Rescue techniques and equipment used: _____

_____

Instructions given: _____

_____

Person released to: Returned to facility   Parent/guardian   EMS   Other: _____

Was EMS notified?   No   Yes, medic(s): _____ Arrival time: _____

Was person transferred?   No   Yes, name of hospital: _____

Person released to: Returned to facility   Parent/guardian   EMS   Other: _____

Was EMS notified?   Not necessary   Yes   Refused (see below)

If EMS was notified, was person transferred?   No   Yes, name of hospital: _____

Signature of rescuer or person completing this report: _____

Printed name of rescuer or person completing this report: _____

Refusal of Care and Acknowledgement of Information

I understand that the basic first aid care provided by the aquatic staff is not a substitute for care by EMS, a physician, or a hospital. I (or minor named above) have been offered one or more of the following services: EMS evaluation, medical care, and transportation; however, I am refusing the services offered. I have been advised and understand the risks and consequences of refusing advanced care and transport, including the fact that delay in treatment could be hazardous to my health and, under certain circumstances, could result in disability or death.

Release of Liability

By signing this form, I am releasing the attending lifeguards, the aquatic facility, and its agents of any liability or medical claims resulting from my decision to refuse the medical care and transport. I have read and understand the "Acknowledgement of Information" and "Release of Liability."

_____   Refused to sign
               Signature

Relationship (if for a child):   Parent   Guardian

From *StarGuard: Best Practices for Lifeguards, Third Edition* by Jill E. White, 2006, Champaign, IL: Human Kinetics.

Appendix C

Sample Wilderness Participant Safety Talk Outline

I. Introduction

Introduce yourself and your staff, then discuss the activity. For example, "We are going to take a swim here." Tell the participants to listen to what you tell them about the activity and site and to think before taking action. Be sure to state that "the responsibility for safety is shared by all participants."

II. Overview of Conditions

Discuss the general physical characteristics of the area and expected weather conditions.

III. Specifics

Provide the following information before beginning the activity:

Define physical site boundaries.

Explain appropriate equipment usage as necessary.

Explain and demonstrate safety signals that will be used.

Describe inherent dangers (e.g., cold water, dark water, obstructions in the water).

Demonstrate proper techniques (e.g., "Enter the water like this.").

Explain what to do in case of an emergency.

IV. Rules

Explain specific rules, including the following:

Enter all water feetfirst.

Wear foot protection at all times.

Avoid running at the waterfront.

Stay in designated areas.

Use the established buddy system or swimmer identification system.

Avoid drinking lake, river, or creek water without proper treatment.

Avoid throwing rocks and other hard materials.

Avoid swimming underwater.

Follow safety signals.

Follow specific policy for emergency lightning procedures.

Follow specific policy for food and drink at the swimming site.

Use of drugs or alcohol is prohibited prior to or during the activity.

V. Participant Responsibility

Ask participants to let you know if they see any hazards, accidents, or safety concerns.

Explain the level of physical involvement, and that it is each person's responsibility to let the group leader know if he or she has any medical or physical conditions that limit his or her abilities. Consider using a statement such as, "We do not want to keep you from participating in the activity. Our concern is to be prepared to help you in the event you need assistance."

Always provide a private time for disclosure.

VI. Closing

Give each person an opportunity to ask questions; do not patronize or dismiss any participant's concerns.

Make participants feel valued and comfortable.

Tell participants that they are welcome to approach you with additional questions or concerns at any time.

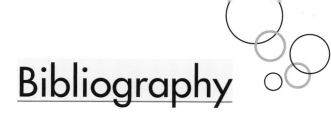

Bibliography

American Academy of Pediatrics Committee on Injury, Violence, and Poison Prevention. 2003, August. Policy statement: Prevention of drowning in infants, children and adolescents. *Pediatrics,* 112(2): 437-439. Retrieved September 9, 2004, from http://pediatrics.aappublications.org/cgi/content/full/112/2/437.

American Heart Association. 2005. Highlights of the 2005 American Heart Association guidelines for cardiopulmonary resuscitation and emergency cardiovascular care. *Currents,* 16: 4. Retrieved November 29, 2005 from www.americanheart.org/eccguidelines.

American Heart Association. 2005. 2005 international consensus on cardiopulmonary resuscitation (CPR) and emergency cardiovascular care (ECC) science with treatment recommendations. *Circulation,* 112: 22 (supplement). Retrived November 28, 2005 from www.circ.ahajournals.org/content/vol112/22_suppl/.

American Heart Association. 2003. International Liaison Committee on Resuscitation (ILCOR) advisory statement: Recommended guidelines for uniform reporting of data from drowning. *Circulation,* 108:2565. Retrieved January 16, 2005, http://circ.ahajournals.org/cgi/content/full/108/20/2565.

American Heart Association. 1990. Advanced cardiac life support (ACLS) subcommittee and emergency cardiac care (ECC) committee medical/scientific statement. Improving survival from sudden cardiac arrest: The "chain of survival" concept. Retrieved April 1, 2005, from http://americanheart.org/presenter.jhtml?identifier=3012022.

American Red Cross. 2004. *Lifeguard training.* Teterboro, NJ: Staywell.

American Safety & Health Institute. 2003. *Basic first aid for the community and workplace.* Holiday, FL: National Instructor's Resource Center.

American Safety & Health Institute. 2003. *Bloodborne pathogens.* Holiday, FL: National Instructor's Resource Center.

American Safety & Health Institute. 2003. *CPR pro.* Holiday, FL: National Instructor's Resource Center.

American Safety & Health Institute and National Academies of Emergency Dispatch. 2002. *Medical emergencies: When to call and what to expect when you dial 9-1-1* (pamphlet). Holiday, FL: ASHI/NAED.

American Safety & Health Institute and Starfish Aquatics Institute. 2000. *Safety training & aquatic rescue/StarGuard.* New Port Ritchie, FL: American Safety & Health Institute.

Auerbach, P. 1995. *Wilderness medicine: Management of wilderness and environmental emergencies.* 3rd ed. St. Louis: Mosby.

Branche, C.M., and S. Stewart, eds. 2001. *Lifeguard effectiveness: A report of the working group.* Retrieved April 10, 2004, from www.cdc.gov/ncipc/lifeguard/LifeguardReport.pdf.

Davis, B. 2005, April. Seeing things clearly. *Aquatics International.* Retrieved April 15, 2005, from www.aquaticsintl.com/2005/apr/0504_rm.html.

DeRosa, S. 2001. 10/20 protection rule: Make it work for you. *From the Stand,* 4(4). Retrieved January 13, 2005, from www.tppc.org/publications_1020.htm.

Drury, J. 1994. *The backcountry classroom.* Merrillville, IN: ICS Books.

Dworkin, G. 2001. *The need for collaborative agreements between fire and rescue agencies and aquatic recreation and lifeguard agencies.* Retrieved November 5, 2003, from www.lifesaving.com/issues/articles/02need_for_collaborative.html.

Ellis, J., and J. White. 1999. *National pool and waterpark lifeguard training.* Sudbury, MA: Jones & Bartlett.

Evans, W. 1995. *Pool aquatic safety: Camp tips.* Glen Allen, VA: Markel Insurance Co.

Fawcett, P. 2005. *Aquatic facility management.* Champaign, IL: Human Kinetics.

Fletemeyer, J., and S. Freas, eds. 1999. *Drowning: New perspectives on intervention and prevention.* Boca Raton, FL: CRC Press.

Forgey, W. 2000. *Wilderness medical society practice guidelines.* Guilford, CT: Globe Pequot Press.

Gookin, J. 2001. *National outdoor leadership school field staff manual.* Lander, WY: National Outdoor Leadership School.

Graydon, D. 1992. *Mountaineering: The freedom of the hills.* 5th ed. Seattle: Moutaineers.

Griffiths, T. 1994. *The complete swimming pool reference.* St. Louis: Mosby.

Griffiths, T. 2002a, January. Lifeguard vigilance: How best to scan. *Aquatics International,* 14(5): 24-27.

Griffiths, T. 2002b, June. A master scan. *Aquatics International* 14(5): 24-27.

Health and Safety Commission and Sport England. 2003. *Managing health and safety in swimming pools* (HSG 179). Sudbury, UK: HSE Books.

International Life Saving Federation. 1998. *Medical Commission's statement on sun dangers for the lifeguard.* Retrieved November 10, 2004, from www.usla.org/PublicInfo/library/ILS_Med_State_SP.pdf.

LaRue, R. 2005, April. Aquatic safety review 3 (ASR3). *CampBusiness.* Retrieved April 14, 2005, from www.camp-business.com/cb0405asr3.html.

Model, J.H., 1999. Etiology and Treatment of Drowning. In *Drowning: New perspectives on intervention and prevention,* edited by J. Fletemeyer and S.J. Freas. Boca Raton, FL: CRC Press.

National Guidelines for First Aid Training in Occupational Settings. 2002. *First aid provider core elements course guide.* 2nd ed. Retrieved February 3, 2005, from www.ngfatos.net/documents.shtml.

National Lightning Safety Institute. 2005. *Indoor/outdoor swimming pool safety.* Retrieved February 19, 2005, from www.lightningsafety.com/nlsi_pls/swimming_pools.html.

Occupational Safety and Health Administration, *Occupational exposure to bloodborne pathogens,* Standard 29 CFR part 1910.1030. Retrieved January 4, 2005, from www.osha.gov/pls/oshaweb/owadisp.show_document?p_table=PREAMBLES&p_id=801.

Pia, F. 1984. The RID factor as a cause of drowning. First published in *Parks & Recreation,* June: 52-67. Retrieved September 10, 2003, from www.pia-enterprises.com/rid.rtf.

Royal Lifesaving Society. 1997. *Pool lifeguard training manual.* St. Louis: Mosby.

Sanders, M. 1995. *Paramedic textbook.* St. Louis: Mosby.

Seiller, B., and R. Shaw. 1995. *Lifeguard vision* (pamphlet). Wheaton, IL: Park District Risk Management Agency.

Skin Cancer Foundation. 2005. *Skin cancer facts.* Retrieved April 27, 2005, from www.skincancer.org/skincancer-facts.php.

Tilton, B. 1998. *The wilderness first responder.* Old Saybrook, CT: Globe Pequot Press.

Tyson, K. and R. Ogoreuc. 2002. STARR: Method for responding to aquatic emergencies. *American Lifeguard.* Winter:15,17,18.

United States Lifesaving Association. 1995. *The USLA manual of open water lifesaving.* Upper Saddle River, NJ: Prentice Hall.

U.S. Department of Health and Human Services Centers For Disease Control and Prevention. 2004. *Fact sheet: Skin cancer: preventing America's most common cancer.* Retrieved October 13, 2004, from www.cdc.gov/cancer/nscpep/about2004.htm.

Westcare Health System. 2001. *Emergency medical services personnel protocols.* Sylva, NC: Westcare Health System.

White, J.E. 2004. *StarGuard pool, waterpark, and waterfront lifeguard training.* Holiday, FL: American Safety & Health Institute.

YMCA of the USA. 2001. *On the guard II: The YMCA lifeguard manual.* Champaign, IL: Human Kinetics.

About the Author

Jill E. White founded the Starfish Aquatics Institute in 2000 with the mission to reduce drowning and save lives by providing reputable, responsive aquatic safety training programs to the public. In 2005 she was named one of the Top 25 Most Influential People in Aquatics by *Aquatics International* magazine, and she has appeared on the US Water Fitness Association's Who's Who in Aquatics: Top 100 Professionals list for the past four years.

© Glamour Shots℠

In the past, White has authored textbooks on lifeguarding, lifeguarding instruction, and swim instruction for the National Safety Council, Jeff Ellis & Associates, and the American Safety & Health Institute. She has firsthand experience in training, supervising, and managing lifeguards and has taught thousands of lifeguards and hundreds of lifeguarding instructors. She has presented educational sessions at conferences for the National Recreation and Park Association; World Waterpark Association; American Alliance for Health, Physical Education, Recreation and Dance; Athletic Business Conference; and numerous state and regional events.

White enjoys reading, hiking, and aquatic sports. She lives in Savannah, Georgia, with her husband, Robbin.

HUMAN KINETICS
The Information Leader in Physical Activity

Starfish Aquatics Institute and Human Kinetics team up to provide outstanding aquatics education and safety courses and resources.

The Rising "STAR" in Aquatic Education

THE BEST LIFEGUARD TRAINING

Protect your patrons and your lifeguards by providing an integrated curriculum of emergency care skills that exceed national standards but with cost and service advantages that keep training time to a minimum!

THE BEST SWIM INSTRUCTION

Teach people to swim for pleasure, fitness, or competition, but teach them correctly through Starfish Swim School! We offer a complete swimming instruction system for all ages and abilities.

RUN A SAFE AND EFFICIENT OPPERATION

The StarReview(tm) program follows the Starfish Risk Management Model, evaluating performance in prevention, surveillance, aquatic rescue, emergency care, and professionalism/personal safety.

RAISE WATER SAFETY AWARENESS

Safety Training and Aquatic Rescue (STAR)® is an awareness level water safety program designed for non-lifeguards such as parents and caregivers, pool and slide attendants, water exercise instructors, health club and resort personnel, and swimming coaches.

PARTNER WITH THE BEST IN THE BUSINESS

The Starfish Aquatics Institute offers a new approach to providing aquatic training and risk management services to aquatic facilities with an all-inclusive program that designates your aquatic facility or agency as a Training Center. There are five levels of Partner Plans to choose from!

Through the new Starfish Aquatic Education Center, Human Kinetics will develop and deliver online courses and associated resources to expand Starfish Aquatics Institute's existing curriculums with courses including:
- StarGuard lifeguard and Starfish Swim School Instructor courses
- Safety Training and Aquatic Rescue (STAR) courses
- Pool Chemistry & Pool Operator course
- Pool Manager course

For more information about Starfish programs please call the national office at 912-692-1173 or visit our web site at www.starfishaquatics.org